Accounting for Managers

2

SELF-DEVELOPMENT FOR MANAGERS

A major new series of workbooks for managers edited by Jane Cranwell-Ward

This series presents a selection of books in workbook format, on a range of key management issues and skills. The books are designed to provide practising managers with the basis for self-development across a wide range of industries and occupations.

Each book relates to other books in the series to provide a coherent new approach to self-development for managers. Closely based on the latest management training initiatives, the books are designed to complement management development programmes, in-house company training, and management qualification programmes such as CMS, DMS, MBA and professional qualification programmes.

Other books in the series:

Thriving on Stress
Jan Cranwell-Ward

Managing Change
Colin Carnall

Effective Problem Solving
Dave Francis

Developing Assertiveness
Anni Townend

The series editor **Jane Cranwell-Ward** is the Director of Company Programmes at Henley – The Management College. She is the author of *Managing Stress* (Pan, 1986).

Accounting for Managers

Roger Oldcorn

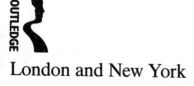

London and New York

First published 1993
by Routledge
11 New Fetter Lane, London EC4P 4EE

Simultaneously published in the USA and Canada
by Routledge
29 West 35th Street, New York, NY 10001

Typeset in Times by Leaper & Gard Ltd, Bristol
Printed and bound in Great Britain by
Biddles Ltd, Guildford and King's Lynn

British Library Cataloguing in Publication Data
A catalogue reference for this book is available from the British Library.

ISBN 0-415-00230-3

Library of Congress Cataloging in Publication Data
has been applied for.

ISBN 0-415-00230-3

Contents

Preface

All managers in the 1990s need at least a basic understanding of accounting so that they can manage budgets and talk intelligently to the finance department. For some managers there is an inbuilt fear when it comes to numbers and understanding company accounts.

Accounting for Managers has been written to introduce the financially inexperienced manager to the techniques used by accountants. The book builds up logically, so readers will need to avoid the temptation of skipping certain chapters.

Having read the book managers will be much better equipped to understand financial documents, to use financial ratios to appraise a business and to contribute more effectively to growing a financially viable business.

Roger Oldcorn was the ideal choice for writing this book. He started his working life as a business economist, has had experience as a consultant and entered management education in the mid 1970s. He has a natural ability for teaching finance, making it both understandable and enjoyable. He is also the author of several books on management and finance.

Jane Cranwell-Ward
Series Editor

Introduction

This book is for managers who have financial responsibilities but who are not specifically trained in accounting and finance and who are not working in the accounting function. It is addressed, therefore, to every manager who has a budget, who spends money and who works in an organisation where money is a scarce resource. The emphasis is on accounting in a business environment, though managers in every type of organisation have a responsibility to operate in a businesslike manner, and that means watching the money side as though it were their own.

The need for a book like this arises because so little time is spent at school on matters financial. As a result, the majority of managers find themselves in a position of financial responsibility without having had much chance to learn about the subject. Unfortunately, all organisations use money, need money and pay wages in money (usually!), and it is a rare and expensive commodity.

Over the years, the art of accounting and finance has grown in complexity as a result of tax laws, company legislation and the growth of business enterprises. Consequently a mass of specialist terminology has emerged, making the subject seem almost a foreign language. In addition many techniques have been invented as aids to good decision-making and for control. The effect has been to create a gulf between those who understand accounting and finance and those who do not.

The gap seems to be widening. The accountants themselves must bear some of the blame; they have to learn to be effective communicators and to go out of their way to comprehend the complex nature of the problems faced by their colleagues in operating management. But operating managers, too, must close the communications gap by being able to speak the language of accountancy and know what the main techniques are. In addition they must be able to ask the right questions and request the right information. This book is designed to help managers do these things.

A book of this size cannot possibly cover all aspects of accounting, and the expert may spot omissions. These are not critical. At the end there is a reading list, and I hope that the reader will be sufficiently interested by the end to want to take up the references.

To get the most out of the book, take a chapter at a time, in sequence – each new topic builds on what has gone before – and take time to try the little exercises for yourself. Have a pencil and paper handy, and a calculator will be useful too. If you find there is something you do not grasp after several attempts, ask a friendly accountant for help (they are usually flattered by such requests).

Finally, in a working context, *use* your accountants; they are there for your benefit (not the other way round), to help you manage the affairs of the organisation efficiently and profitably.

1   *Business aims*

In this chapter we are going to look at the question of what the aims of a business might be and to consider the concept of profit – what it is and why it is important. We also need to think about the difference between profit and cash. In addition, the idea of wealth will be explained: what it is and where it comes from.

Consider the following two (related) questions:

- Why does a business exist?
- What is its purpose?

What would your answers be? The words that spring to mind might relate to freedom and independence (if the business you are thinking about is small and family-owned). The words might relate to providing a service or products that people want (if the business is a 'marketing-orientated' enterprise). Or the words might be related to money – for example to becoming wealthy or rich or big (if viewed from a shareholder or investor perspective).

There are other reasons why firms exist. Companies are started because people wish to achieve something, solve a problem, develop an invention, become powerful or famous. But underlying all of them there is an assumption that money is involved and that somehow without it the company will cease to exist – it will go broke. Often the idea of creating wealth is there too; making enough money to make the firm, its staff and its owners better off than before.

At the end of the day, the firm has to be able to sell enough of something at the right price, to be able to make a sufficient profit to enable it to continue in business tomorrow. Later, we need to look at what these phrases mean: 'sell enough'; 'right price'; 'sufficient profit'. For now, we need to look more closely at the word 'profit' and work out what that means.

EXERCISE: THE CASE OF THE FIVE SIMPLE BUSINESSES

Here are five business situations. Each relates to a month's trading activity by the owners of small firms:

- Albert buys 1,000 cans of paint for £2.00 each and sells them for £1.80 each.
- Bill buys 1,000 cans of paint for £2.00 and offers them for sale at £20.00.
- Charlie buys 50,000 cans of paint for £1.90 a can (he gets a quantity discount of 10p a can) and sells 1,000 at £2.50.
- Dan buys 1,500 cans of paint for £2.00 each and sells them all at £2.50, but takes 'IOU's' from his customers instead of cash. (The customers say they will pay next month.)
- Eddie buys 1,000 cans of paint at £2.00 each and sells them all for cash for £2.50.

Which of the five businessmen do you think has the best chance of being successful?

Albert's business will be popular – selling paint at less than cost is always welcomed by customers. But I wonder how long he can continue to lose money at the rate of £200 a month? Apart from anything else, where is the money coming from? Who supplies that?

Bill's business sounds interesting. If he can sell paint for £20.00 a can he will be making £18.00 profit on every can he sells – £1,800 a month! But how many cans of paint do you think he will sell at that price? Not very many!

Charlie is a great buyer. He takes advantage of quantity discounts. Unfortunately for him he cannot sell his stock – in fact it will take him over four years to shift all the cans of paint in his warehouse. Moreover, he had to pay the supplier for the goods he ordered – £95,000. Yet he received only £2,500 from sales. He must either be a very rich paint dealer or have a very friendly bank manager.

Dan, in contrast, is a great seller. He is generous to his customers, allowing them to take time to pay. So they like to buy from him. Unfortunately, he has probably had to pay the supplier £3,000 for the paint delivered. Like Albert and Charlie, he has to find the money from somewhere else.

What about Eddie? Boring, conservative, cautious – but he is making money and does not appear to need to borrow any.

If we had to choose one of these five, Eddie's operation is the one that has the best chance of success, because it is making a profit and is financially sound. Dan's might work if he has money behind him, but the others are all a bit odd.

PROFIT DEFINED

These examples will be referred to often in this book because they represent situations (rather exaggerated) that frequently arise in business. Also they illustrate nicely the two fundamental principles of business finance:

- the meaning of *profit*;
- the difference between *profit* and *cash*.

What is profit?

Profit is the *difference* between the value of what is *sold* and the *costs* which may be reasonably attributed to those sales.

It is *not* the difference between cash sales and all costs, nor the difference between sales and the cost of purchases or the cost of what has been made.

EXERCISE

Now work out how much profit each of the five businessmen made using the numbers given above. Assume that there were no other expenses and no other income. Also assume that Bill actually managed to sell just one can of paint (at £20). Fill in your answers below, then look at the way the correct answers have been calculated.

	Profit (£)
Albert	....
Bill	....
Charlie	....
Dan	....
Eddie	....

Here are the correct figures and the way they have been calculated:

EXAMPLE

	Cans sold	Profit per can (£)	Profit (£)
Albert	1,000	loss 0.20	loss 200
Bill	1	18.00	18
Charlie	1,000	0.60	600
Dan	1,500	0.50	750
Eddie	1,000	0.50	500

Which business would you think is the best? If profit is the only criterion of success, then the prize goes to Dan, who made most profit. Clearly Albert has a problem. Bill's performance is feeble; the other two are not far behind Dan.

EXERCISE

Now look at the cash position of our five paint salesmen. Work out how much cash they would have at the end if they all started out with a zero bank balance:

	(£)
Albert	....
Bill	....
Charlie	....
Dan	....
Eddie	....

In many ways the cash situation is a lot easier to work out. The balance at the end of the trading period is simply the difference between the money which came in and the money which went out. These are usually referred to as *receipts* and *payments*. So:

Receipts less payments equals cash.

EXAMPLE

	Receipts (£)	Payments (£)	Cash (£)
Albert	1,800	2,000	−200
Bill	20	2,000	−1,980
Charlie	2,500	95,000	−92,500
Dan	0	3,000	−3,000
Eddie	2,500	2,000	500

Which is the better business now?

If you compare cash and profit figures for the five, they all have different profiles and in only one case are the cash and profit figures the same amount. Remember:

Profit and cash are not the same thing in business, but you need both!

WHAT ABOUT WEALTH?

Which of our five businessmen would be the wealthiest at the end of the month? One way to decide would be to use the profit figure alone. Clearly Dan comes out top with £750. Unfortunately he also owes £3,000, but so long as his customers pay up and he can clear his debts then he will truly be £750 better off. This is the wealth he has created and in business it is often called *net worth* or *equity capital* and it comes about by retaining profits in the business.

SUMMARY OF CHAPTER

■ Profit is the difference between the value of what is sold and relevant costs.
■ Profit and cash are rarely the same in business.
■ Wealth is determined by the size of the profits put back into the business.

2 Costs, sales and profit

This chapter looks more closely at costs and how they are dealt with in the accounts. In addition, the way profit can be described needs a closer inspection – it is open to many interpretations.

In the last chapter we had the example of five small firms selling paint. One of the more successful was Eddie's: he managed to sell 1,000 cans at a profit of 50p a can, clearing out his stock entirely and making a profit for the month, in total, of £500. We assumed that there were no other costs, but in reality he would undoubtedly have incurred other expenses.

EXERCISE

> What other costs would a trader like Eddie normally have incurred? In the space below create a list of possible expenses or costs (seven or eight items will do):

Here is a list of the more typical items to be included in a list of costs:

- wages and salaries;
- pension and social security payments;

- van fuel and oil;
- van repairs and maintenance;
- heat, light;
- telephone and postage;
- stationery;
- rent and rates;
- insurance;
- advertising;
- bank charges.

Often many of these items are known as *overheads*, and it is usual to divide the wage and salary costs between different activities. This results in some costs being classified *departmentally*. For instance, if Eddie employs a salesman and has someone in an office, the total wage bill might be split into 'selling costs' and 'administration'.

SOME SPECIAL COSTS

- Most companies have their accounts checked by independent accountants. This is the *audit*, and the auditors are legally responsible to the owners (whether or not these are called shareholders). The audit fee is a cost all firms bear.
- If a company owns an asset which lasts over a year – say a building or a machine – then any reduction in its value is considered to be a *cost*. This cost is *depreciation* – more on this in Chapter 3.
- In addition to bank charges, many firms borrow money and the interest they pay is a cost which needs to be highlighted.

THE PROFIT AND LOSS ACCOUNT

At the end of the financial year, all firms have to produce a statement showing how much profit has been made, taking into consideration sales, the cost of sales and all other costs. Companies that have *limited liability* (they will have 'Ltd' or 'PLC' after the name) are legally obliged to produce a *profit and loss account*. All firms have to produce accounts annually for the taxman and all should produce accounts at regular intervals – preferably monthly – for the managers.

Limited liability simply means that if the company fails, the shareholders can only lose the money they have already invested in the business; they cannot be held liable for more.

A full profit and loss account might look like this:

EXAMPLE

Eddie's Paints Ltd
Profit and Loss Account
Year ending 31 December 1999

	£
Sales	30,000
Less: Cost of sales	24,000
Gross profit	6,000
Less: Selling costs	1,500
Administration	2,500
Operating profit	2,000
Plus: Interest receivable	10
Less: Interest payable	60
Profit before tax	1,950
Less: Corporation Tax	450
Profit after tax	£1,500

(handwritten annotation: trading account)

Important items to note

- The word 'profit' is used in four different places; if you were asked 'How much profit did the firm make?' you would be perfectly justified in answering: 'What sort of profit are you talking about?' (In fact there is a fifth, hidden figure; it is 'profit before interest and tax' i.e. £2,010: operating profit + interest received.)
- The phrase 'operating profit' is often replaced by 'trading profit', and an account which ends at that line is termed 'the trading account'.
- Net profit after tax is often called 'earnings after tax' and in the USA you will find the expression 'net income'.

EXERCISE

What can a company do with the net profit after tax it has earned? There are only two things a firm can do with its earnings:

■   Pay it out to the owners (shareholders). This is called a *dividend*.

■   Keep it in the firm. This is called *retained profit* or *retained earnings*.

By retaining profits the firm is able to acquire more assets, and is thus enabled to grow.

PUBLISHED ACCOUNTS VERSUS INTERNAL ACCOUNTS

The accounting information companies have to publish is set out in the Companies Acts (in Britain). Also the Stock Market has certain disclosure requirements, and the accounting profession has standards too. These are known as 'SSAPs' (Statements of Standard Accounting Practice). The recently formed Accounting Standards Board will gradually replace many SSAPs with clearer, often tougher, rules. These are known as Financial Reporting Standards (FRSs).

The profit and loss account shown on page 9 contains most of the information that has to be published annually. In addition, in Britain, the accounts must show, in relation to the profit and loss account, *inter alia*:

■   dividend payments;
■   depreciation charges;
■   auditors' fees;
■   total wage and salary cost;
■   directors' wages and fees (often referred to as 'emoluments');
■   charitable and political contributions;
■   all exceptional and extraordinary costs or income.

Do you think that this information is sufficient (or frequent enough) to enable the company's managers to exercise proper control over its affairs?

The general view is that these accounts are 'too little and too late' and that much more detail, produced regularly and fast, is necessary for proper control. We will have a closer look at these matters in Chapters 7, 8 and 9.

SUMMARY OF CHAPTER

■ The word 'profit' is meaningless on its own; several levels of profit can be described.

■ Many different types of cost will be found in any business and it is possible to divide them up by department or function.

■ Depreciation of assets is a loss of value and this is a cost 'against the profits'.

■ Net profit after tax is used for dividends to the owners, or ploughed back to enable the business to grow.

3 *Assets and their valuation*

The aim of this chapter is to review the types of asset that can be found in a business enterprise. We will look at what these assets are, and how there are often problems when it comes to putting a value on them.

ASSETS: A DEFINITION

Assets are things of value owned by an organisation.

EXERCISE

Think of a company you know well, your local supermarket or garage, for instance. At any given time it will have items of value that it has purchased. How many can you think of in two minutes?

Here is a list of the different types of asset to be found in many companies, together with some notes about each one. Usually assets are listed in a document called the *balance sheet* which has to be prepared annually and which shows their current values, assuming the firm is a *going concern* (i.e. not going broke). The items on your list will probably be found here somewhere, although you may have used different words:

- Cash – at the bank or 'in hand'.
- Investments – money on deposit, government bonds or shares in other companies.
- Stocks – sometimes called inventories. These include materials, goods held for resale (as on a supermarket shelf), finished products, and work in progress (partly completed items). A builder will often have a stock of land held for development at a later date.
- Debtors – or receivables. The value of money owed to the company by customers (unlikely in a supermarket which sells everything for cash only).

Those assets are called *current assets.*

- Land – if the firm owns land it is an important asset.
- Buildings.
- Machinery and equipment; special kinds of equipment like boilers, cranes and lifts are often called 'plant'.
- Cars, vans, furniture.

Those assets are called *fixed assets.*

TANGIBLE AND INTANGIBLE ASSETS

All the assets described above are referred to as tangible assets, but there are other kinds of asset which are less easily identifiable and these we refer to as *intangibles.* The best example is the asset called *goodwill.*

GOODWILL DEFINED

Goodwill is the difference between the price paid to acquire a business (or part of a business) and the value of the tangible assets acquired.

EXERCISE

> If we bought a small hotel for £2 million, the value of the land, buildings, equipment and furniture, and the stock in trade might be £1.5 million. In this case we have paid £500,000 for the goodwill of the business.
>
> What have you bought with the £500,000?

Items you might possibly have acquired would include – the name of the pub, its reputation, a customer base, and the staff. But most of all you have bought the prospect of a stream of profits in the future (for ever!).

THE INTANGIBLE ASSET PROBLEM

Traditionally in Britain goodwill has usually been omitted from the accounts by 'writing off' the value on acquisition, so that the amount would not be seen anywhere in the firm's accounts other than by way of a footnote. The reason is that since the asset is intangible and is a payment for future profits, its value could diminish – even disappear – at any time. This practice seems sensible, bearing in mind the need to be prudent and to show only realistic values for assets.

In contrast, in the USA and in many other countries, goodwill is included in the accounts as an asset; some British firms are now also preparing their accounts in this way, arguing that goodwill is a real value which should be shown – and maybe revalued (up or down) from time to time.

If you want to see how this works in practice, look at recent accounts of Bass PLC (which has written off goodwill) and Grand Metropolitan PLC (which has left it in).

One or two companies have gone further and created values even though there has been no purchase. Rank, Hovis McDougall PLC is the best known example. It had many brand names which, it believed, were valuable and which the takeover company (Tomkins) had to pay for in 1992. The value had been built up over the years and so a 'brand valuation' was undertaken annually, the resulting values appearing in the balance sheet as assets.

This is highly controversial. What do you think? Should firms leave the valuation in or leave it out?

VALUING ASSETS

Suppose you bought a typewriter in 1980 for £30. How much would it be worth today? Your answer might well depend on how useful it is to you now. If it is worn out, obsolete and on the scrapheap, its value would be virtually nothing. If, however, it is in perfect condition, or essential, then its value may be higher.

All assets have to be valued; the problem lies in deciding on that value.

Three guiding principles

■ The firm is a going concern.
■ The way you value has to be consistent, year after year.
■ You value prudently.

Current assets are usually valued *at cost*, in other words at the price which was paid for them, or reflecting the costs that have been spent on them.

EXERCISE: A STOCK VALUATION PROBLEM

In Chapter 1 five different business situations were described. At the end of the month, two of the paint sales firms were left with stock in hand – Bill who sold only one can at £20.00, leaving him with 999 cans in store (which he paid £2.00 a can for), and Charlie who bought his for £1.90 but was left with 49,000 in store at the end, having sold 1,000 at £2.50 each.

What value would you put on the cans of paint in Bill's and Charlie's stores?

Normally, the cans of paint would be valued at the price that was paid for them. In Bill's case this was £2.00 and in Charlie's case £1.90. They are not valued at selling price, as this would be taking a profit before it had been earned.

Charlie's situation is a bit odd. He might decide that he had no hope of selling such a huge pile of paint unless something dramatic was done. If he decided he could only get rid of the paint by selling at £1.80 a can, then the value of his stock would be just £1.80 a can.

The rule is:

Stocks are valued at cost or at net realisable value, whichever is the lower.

'Realisable value' means 'what you can get for it'.

VALUING FIXED ASSETS

With most fixed assets (except land) it is assumed that the value will diminish over time. This loss of value is called *depreciation*, and as we saw in the last chapter is a cost to the company and comes off its profits.

Why do assets lose their value?

Three basic causes of depreciation

- Wear and tear (things get worn out with use).
- Obsolescence (things become out-of-date or old-fashioned).
- Age (second-hand assets are not as valuable as brand-new ones).

Remember this all relates to commercial assets, not to antiques, works of art, vintage cars, and such-like.

ACCOUNTING TREATMENT OF DEPRECIATION

The commonest method of depreciating an asset is known as *straight-line depreciation*. These are the steps in determining it:

- Estimate the useful life of the asset.
- Decide if there will be any value at the end of this period (what is called 'residual value').
- The difference between purchase price and residual value is the

amount to be written off over the life of the asset.
■ It is assumed that the loss of value is a permanent loss.

Example of depreciation

Eddie bought a van for £5,000. He estimated it would last four years and would be worth £200 at the end.

The total to be depreciated was £4,800 over four years, or £1,200 a year. This is 25 per cent per annum. The sum of £1,200 was therefore deducted from his profits every year for four years and the value of the asset was shown in his books at £1,200 a year less each year:

■ End year 1: value £3,800.
■ End year 2: value £2,600.
■ End year 3: value £1,400.
■ End year 4: value £200.

If Eddie had decided that the asset was only going to last for three years, then the depreciation would have been £1,600 a year. His profits would have been £400 a year less!

Another reason why profit and cash are always different is because capital expenditure (buying assets) is not a cost to set against profit. Only the fraction of the price of the asset that equals its depreciation is included as a cost.

ASSET LIFE

The number of years an asset is expected to be useful varies from asset to asset and from firm to firm. There are some general conventions, however:

■ Buildings: 40 to 100 years.
■ Ships: 20 to 40 years.
■ Machinery: 3 to 15 years.
■ Vehicles: 3 to 7 years.

There are many exceptions, and in the published accounts of companies you will find a note stating what rates of depreciation have been used.

LAND VALUATION

What is the expected life of a piece of land in the middle of London? What rate of depreciation should be charged?

The answers are that the life of land is 'for ever' (usually) and therefore no depreciation is chargeable. Instead, land tends to appreciate in value in the long run, because of inflation and shortage. So these days companies tend to revalue land, and often buildings, from time to time.

Note that a building's value can be appreciating and depreciating at the same time, because the market value may be rising – even though it is losing value through wear and tear or obsolescence; the same may apply to equipment in times of high inflation rates.

ACCOUNTING FOR APPRECIATION OF ASSETS

Unlike depreciation, which is charged against profits, the *increase* in value of an asset (appreciation) is shown as an increase in the underlying value of the business. It makes the 'worth' of the company greater.

Why revalue your assets?

Can you think of any good reasons why companies should go to all the bother and expense of having their assets revalued?

There are several reasons for keeping the value of your assets at up-to-date values:

- The accounts are supposed to reflect 'true' values.
- Having higher values gives greater borrowing powers.
- It makes the shareholders' investment worth more.
- Undervalued assets make the firm cheaper and thus an easier take-over target.
- If your assets are undervalued, you may look more profitable than you really are. For example:
  - Asset bought in 1960 for   £10,000
  - Profit thereon in 1993   £1,000
  - Return on assets in 1993   10%
  - Assets revalued in 1993 to £20,000
  - Revised return on assets   5%

Which of the two return-on-assets figures (10 per cent or 5 per cent) do you think gives the truer picture of the company's profitability?

SUMMARY OF CHAPTER

■ Current assets are short-term in nature, whereas fixed assets are held for longer periods of time.

■ There is debate currently as to whether intangible assets like goodwill should be written off on acquisition or kept as assets of value. Brand valuations are also the subject of fierce debate.

■ Stocks are valued at cost or net realisable value, whichever is the lower.

■ Fixed assets are depreciated; this does not apply to land.

■ Depreciation rates vary, but are intended to reflect the loss of value of an asset.

■ Asset appreciation is also undertaken from time to time by many companies for various reasons.

4 Sources of finance

In this chapter we will look at the different ways in which companies can raise money.

In the last chapter we discussed assets – things of value in the business which will enable it to trade and make a profit. The question now is: 'Where do firms get the money from to be able to buy all these assets?' There are several important sources.

OWNERS' CAPITAL

Most small firms start in the same way. The owner or owners put into the business some, or all, of their own money. This is called the *capital employed* of the firm, and the money so invested is used to buy assets of one type or another.

If the company is set up as a limited company and decides to issue shares, what happens in effect is that in exchange for parting with their money, the owners receive a piece of paper called a 'share certificate' stating that they have a share in the ownership of the firm.

EXAMPLE: RAISING SHARE CAPITAL

Suppose our five famous paint salesmen decided to form a company and pool their efforts. They agreed that the share capital would be £25,000 and each would contribute as much as he wished. They decided that each share would have a nominal value of 25p and so the company would have to 'sell' to them a total of 100,000 shares.

- Albert bought 20,000 at a cost of £5,000
- Bill bought 10,000 at a cost of   £2,500
- Charlie bought 15,000 for   £3,750
- Dan bought 25,000 for   £6,250
- Eddie bought 30,000 for   £7,500

They are all shareholders of the Company and as such are owners of it. They are entitled to vote at meetings of the company, each share carries one vote.

The capital of the company is known as *share capital* or *equity capital* ('the equity') and sometimes the expression used is 'risk capital', because if the company fails they will lose the money they have invested. They will only get it back if the assets of the firm turn out to be worth more than the firm's debts.

Why invest?

Why do people bother to invest their money in shares if all that may happen is they lose it?

There are two main financial reasons for investing in the equity of companies (ignoring speculative investing):

- If the company makes a profit the shareholders might reasonably expect to receive some of it as a dividend. *All* profit is theirs, but companies keep back some rather than give it away, as we saw in Chapter 2 (see page 10).
- If the underlying worth of the company rises, then the value of the shares will be higher. This is the 'wealth creation' process we discussed in Chapter 1.

LOANS

Loans to companies both large and small are common. It is a very different means of financing a business from equity or share capital. With small firms, loans are often from relatives of the owners; with larger companies banks provide a large amount; but there are ways of borrowing huge sums from individuals as well. All loans are referred to as *loan capital* or *borrowed capital* and sometimes the word *liabilities* is used. A more descriptive word is 'debt'.

The three essential features of loans

If you were invited to lend money to a company and you were told all about the company's business, what would you need to know before committing yourself (assuming you had the money to lend)?

The three essential questions to have answered are:

1   For how long is the loan going to be made? Some individuals or institutions may only be prepared to lend for a couple of years, others may wish, or be able, to take a very long-term view (e.g. life assurance companies).

2   What rate of interest is being offered? Not many people would be tempted to lend money if the rate of interest is going to be smaller than alternative, similar investments.

3   Is there any guarantee that the money lent will be safe? Of course, investing in business enterprises cannot be 100 per cent risk-free. However, often a loan is made to a business with the guarantee that an asset 'belongs' to the lender. This is the 'security' for the loan. The majority of loans are called 'secured loans', though you will find some called 'unsecured loans'.

These three conditions apply to all borrowed money. The three key words to remember are:

■ Time
■ Interest
■ Security

How does each of these three features differ when comparing loan capital with equity capital?

EXAMPLE *(shares)*

	Equity	*Loans*
Time:	For ever	Limited
Interest:	Only paid if there is a profit (as a dividend)	Agreed at the start, often fixed
Security:	None (at risk)	Against the assets

SOURCES OF LOAN MONEY

Money from banks

Banks in Britain traditionally lend to companies rather than investing in equities directly; this is unlike the practice in Japan. A bank loan will have to be secured against an asset, it will be for a specific period of time and the bank will state the rate of interest to be paid. This may be fixed over a period of the loan, or expressed as a certain number of percentage points above the bank's base lending rate (strong and well-established firms get better rates than those with no track record or poor credit-ratings) – a variable rate. The two main types of bank loan are:

- An overdraft, which is really a way of helping the company to continue paying its normal bills even if not much money is coming in. For example, the owner of a seaside hotel may need to carry out some major repairs before the season starts. An overdraft would be helpful in such a situation.
- A medium-term loan, which is used to pay for a specific asset like a new machine or a car.

Money from financial institutions

Many organisations can provide finance for companies and are collectively called 'financial institutions'. Insurance companies, in particular, lend money to firms; often the loans are of a long-term nature. Security is usually property and as such can be classified as 'mortgage loans'.

Bonds and things

The 1980s saw a dramatic rise in the use of bonds as a means of borrowing money. The buyer of a bond receives a fixed rate of interest and eventually the company repays the loan, often many years after its issue. Bonds issued by large companies are traded on stock markets, just like ordinary shares. One type of bond is a 'preference share', which is sometimes considered to be 'almost equity capital', but which gives the owner preference over the ordinary shareholder in receiving a dividend.

To see just how much borrowing large companies do, get hold of the Annual Report and Accounts of a few well-known companies. Some borrow very little, but others will have many different types of loan, at different rates of interest and with different repayment dates.

Suppliers as a source of finance

To say that money can be obtained from suppliers is not entirely accurate. What happens is that a company delays paying its bills and so has use of its money a little longer than it should. This type of financing is called 'creditors' or, in the USA, 'bills payable'. For some types of business the use of creditors as a source of finance is a key factor in the way they operate. For example, the big retail stores all obtain goods from their suppliers on credit, put the goods on the shelves, sell them for cash and hang onto the money for a few weeks. Only then are the suppliers paid. This can lead to cash-flow problems in supplier companies. As a result the 1992 Budget in Britain took a significant step to alleviate the problem, indicating that a 30-day payment period should be adhered to in relation to government contracts.

The difficulty for companies with a slow payment policy is that the supplier may cease to want to do business with them. Small firms are particularly at risk from this. However, very big companies get away with it because the suppliers do not want to lose the business.

Other creditors

Apart from trade creditors, most companies find that they owe money but have a while before cash has to be paid out. In particular, corporation tax on profits is not due to be paid until after the end of the year; and dividends, too, are not paid until well after the end of the year to which they relate. In both instances, the company has use of the money in the interim.

Finance from customers

We all have sometimes to pay for a product or service before we receive it. You can probably think of several examples immediately – a holiday, a concert ticket, a subscription to a journal. In all these cases the company has use of your money before it delivers the goods or service. Occasionally the company goes bust before delivering, and then folks get hurt.

RETAINED PROFITS

Once a business has got going and, with any luck, is making a profit, the main source of finance is that generated by the business itself in the form of profits. As long as the company does not pay out all the after-tax profits as dividends, what is left will be ploughed back into the business and is an addition to the equity capital of the firm.

Retained earnings are used to buy more assets. In the past, these retained earnings were always called 'reserves'; but this suggests a pile of cash in the safe, which is not correct. The cash involved will have been used to buy other assets.

RIGHTS ISSUES

From time to time a company may decide it needs more finance but prefers not to borrow. Instead it can sell more shares, and the usual method is by offering existing shareholders the right to buy additional ordinary shares in the firm. It may offer shares on the open market, but it has to obtain shareholder approval first.

The company will decide how much it needs to raise and will then offer extra shares to existing shareholders, usually at a discount to the existing share price. These shares are offered pro rata to the shareholders' existing holding.

EXAMPLE

Harry's Ltd has a share capital of 10 million ordinary shares with a nominal value of 10p a share. The current market price is £3.50 a share, and the company needs to raise an extra £3 million. The offer to existing shareholders might be 1 for 10 already held at £3.00 each.

Thus an extra 1 million shares would be sold, raising £3 million, which is an addition to the company's equity capital. The share price of the company would fall to £3.45 as a result:

1 The original market value was £35 million (10 million shares at £3.50).
2 The sale raises £3 million (1 million shares at £3.00).

3   The total market value is now £38 million for 11 million shares.
4   This gives an average value per share of £3.45 (approximately).

SUMMARY OF CHAPTER

There are three basic sources of finance:

■ selling shares;
■ retaining profits.

These two are called Equity capital or shareholders' funds; and the third source is:

■ borrowings.

All borrowed money is called *debt* and may be long-term, such as bonds or mortgage loans, or short-term, mainly from trade creditors and bank overdrafts.

5 Working capital management

This chapter deals with an essential element of good business management – making sure that the firm has adequate funds to carry on business. Many small firms, especially, fail because of a failure to manage working capital.

WHAT IS WORKING CAPITAL?

Working capital is concerned with the day-to-day financial operations of a business and the problem of ensuring that there is enough cash in the firm to be able to pay what is owed – and still continue to trade.

Look back at Chapter 1. The five business examples we studied were all situations with different working capital problems.

THE ACCOUNTING DEFINITION

- *Working capital* is: current assets less current liabilities.
- *Current assets* are:
  – stocks (including work in progress);
  – debtors;
  – cash and other short-term investments.
- *Current liabilities* are: all sums owed by the firm which have to be paid within a year (e.g. trade creditors, bank overdrafts etc.).

HOW WORKING CAPITAL WORKS

A firm buys a quantity of goods which it intends to sell on later at a profit. Thus its cash falls, but it has stock in hand.

The goods are subsequently sold on credit terms at a profit. Further purchases are made – but the firm may not pay for these purchases immediately – it may hold onto the invoice, especially if it is a little short of cash.

Eventually the customers pay up and the firm can use the cash to pay what it owes – and be able to buy even more goods.

WHY IS THERE A PROBLEM?

The firm may not be able to get its hands on enough cash when the supplier asks for payment. The problem is often compounded by high stock levels (including work in progress), low profit margins and a fast rate of sales growth.

THE ACCOUNTING EQUATION

Stocks + debtors + cash = creditors + borrowings + equity capital

Therefore if you wish to buy more stock, your cash goes down, or you borrow more, or you extend your creditors, or you put in more equity.

If your customers do not pay up (i.e. there is an increase in debtors), you cut stocks, or your cash balances fall, or your overdraft rises, or you put more money in.

EXERCISE

A car dealer buys ten cars a month at £9,000 each, paying for them on the last day of the month. He sells them for £10,000 each. In January this year he sold eight cars only, leaving two cars in stock. He received payment for only six cars and had therefore two debtors on his books. He paid his supplier for eight cars only, ending up owing for two. He started the year with a zero bank balance.

Work out what the accounts of the firm would look like at the end of January. (There are a few clues included to help.)

The accounting items at the end of January are:

	£
Stocks (2 cars @ £9,000)	
Debtors (2 cars @ £10,000)	
Cash	NIL
Total	
Creditors (2 cars @ £9,000)	
Overdraft*	
Profit & loss a/c (8 cars @ £1,000)**	
Total	

Helpline: the totals should both be £38,000.

*The overdraft will be the difference between the cash the dealer received and the cash he paid out in the month. He sold for cash only six cars at £10,000. Therefore he received £60,000. He paid the supplier for eight cars at £9,000; a total of £72,000.

**Where did the *profit* figure come from? He buys at £9,000 and sells for £10,000. A profit of £1,000 is made on every car he sells.

You may argue that the overdraft of £12,000 is nothing to worry about. After all, the dealer has only to sell the two cars in stock or get the money in from the debtors and all the problems are over. The interest charge for a month on the overdraft will be less than £200. So why worry?

EXERCISE: THE EFFECT OF A SALES INCREASE

Work out what would have happened if the business had been double the size it was last January:

- ■ Double the purchases to twenty cars.
- ■ Double sales and profits to sixteen cars.
- ■ Double the stocks to four cars.
- ■ Double the debtors to four cars.

But suppose the firm cannot double its creditors and has to pay for all but two cars.

What happens to the overdraft? Doubled? Less than double? More than double?

Your calculations should have looked like this:

EXAMPLE

	£
Stocks (4 cars @ £9,000)	36,000
Debtors (4 cars @ £10,000)	40,000
Cash	NIL
Total	76,000
Creditors (2 cars @ £9,000)	18,000
Overdraft	42,000
Profit & loss a/c (16 cars @ £1,000)	16,000
Total	76,000

Do you suppose the bank would lend £42,000? The interest charge is now very high. The business has a big problem!
    What do we conclude?

In time of rapid growth (or in inflationary times) high levels of working capital cause acute cash-flow problems.

HOW TO PREVENT A CASH FLOW CRISIS

What would you do in the situation described above?
    One common way of dealing with this sort of problem is to extend one's creditors. In other words, not to pay the suppliers

until the very last minute. This is an all too common practice and it results in suppliers either raising their prices or refusing to do business with you.

Better ways are reducing stock levels, getting in customers' accounts outstanding and raising profit levels.

Stock reduction

Ideally a firm should have just enough in store to satisfy tomorrow's demand – whether this is customer demand or, in a factory, production line needs. This is a 'just-in-time' system and theoretically is ideal. In reality there are many problems, but the aim is sound. Cutting stock levels once they are high is often difficult, unless sales are made at a discount.

Debtor reduction

Firms must always seek to get their money in from customers as fast as possible. Terms should be clearly established before the sale is made; afterwards, the moment the money is overdue, the customer must be contacted – and pursued until they pay. If all else fails, the debtors may be *factored*, which effectively means receiving most of the money owed – but at a price, naturally.

Raising profits

The more profit a firm makes, the greater will be the funds available to pay for an increase in working capital. However, an adequate profit line does not imply that control of working capital is irrelevant; this must always be in the minds of operating managers in everything they do.

SUMMARY OF THE CHAPTER

■ A company with tight control of working capital – its stock levels and its debtors especially – will be able to finance growth far more easily than a company which ties up all its money in these items.

■ Growth for such a firm will be very expensive and can easily result in failure.

6 *The main accounting documents*

This chapter provides an overview of the main accounting documents that are publicly available and the main internal documents that should be available to managers.

PUBLISHED ACCOUNTS

The three main documents which companies have to publish in Britain are:

- the profit and loss account;
- the balance sheet;
- the cash-flow statement.

PROFIT AND LOSS ACCOUNT

The elements of the profit and loss account were described in Chapter 2 (page 9). Remember that the amount of information shown is limited, and therefore care must be taken when interpreting the account. The bottom line of the account will show how much of earnings is paid out as a dividend, and, therefore, how much has been retained in the firm. The old term for these retained earnings is 'reserves'. Also it is usual to show the amount of dividend per share to be paid and the *earnings per share* (EPS) too.

Earnings per share defined

This is profit after tax divided by the average number of ordinary shares in issue during the year. Sometimes the expression 'fully diluted' also appears. This will occur if the company has some 'convertible' loans outstanding. These will be turned into ordinary shares at a later date, so a second EPS is calculated by dividing earnings by what the number of shares will be after the convertibles have been 'converted'.

THE BALANCE SHEET

The balance sheet simply lists all the assets of the firm and the sources of money which have been used to pay for those assets. There are a variety of formats in existence; here are a few:

EXAMPLE A

Capital and liabilities	(£000)	Assets	(£000)
Share capital and reserves	150	Fixed assets	160
Long-term debt	50	Current assets	240
Current liabilities	200		—
Total capital employed	400	Total assets	400

This is sometimes called the 'traditional format' and may be shown, alternatively, with the assets on the right-hand side, and the capital and liabilities items to the left:

EXAMPLE B

Assets	(£000)	Capital and liabilities	(£000)
Current assets	240	Current liabilities	200
Fixed assets	160	Long-term debt	50
	—	Share capital and reserves	150
Total assets	400	Total capital employed	400

This is the layout most often found in North America, though you will notice that the items on each side are not listed in the same way.

Most companies lay out their accounts nowadays in a vertical format, thus:

EXAMPLE C

		£000
Fixed assets		160
Current assets	240	
Less: creditors falling due within one year (i.e. current liabilities)	200	
Net current assets		40
Total assets less current liabilities		200
Less: creditors falling due after one year (i.e. long-term borrowings)		50
Net assets		150
Shareholders' funds		150

The important feature to notice about this balance sheet is that all the items are the same as in the previous illustrations, but the working capital part is highlighted, something impossible with the traditional formats – that is, current assets less current liabilities (or *net current assets*).

EXERCISE

If you obtain a copy of the accounts of a company you know, you will most likely find that its balance sheet is in this format (if it is British). It is a useful exercise to redraw the statement in the traditional format as described above (Examples A and B).

CASH-FLOW STATEMENT

Until recently, published accounts presented a statement called 'the source and application of funds'. This has been replaced by the cash-flow statement, which has a similar aim: namely, to show where the company's cash came from during the year – and what it did with it. The statement brings together elements of the balance sheet and the profit and loss account, so that a difference between the value at the beginning and the end of the year in the item 'Cash in hand and at the bank' is accounted for.

CASH FLOW ILLUSTRATED

From Chapter 1 you will recall that a very important principle of business finance is that profit and cash are different. Here is a case for you to consider about a small firm which started the year with £5,000 in the bank and ended up owing £5,000 to the bank – and made a profit in the meantime. You may wish to work out for yourself where the money went, before looking at the cash-flow statement! Here is the balance sheet at the start of the year:

EXAMPLE

Cashly and Company Ltd
Balance sheet at 1st January 1991

Assets	£	Capital	£
Fixed assets	4,000	Trade creditors	3,500
Stocks	2,500	Taxation	1,500
Debtors	1,300	Bank overdraft	–
Cash	5,000	Current liabilities	5,000
Total assets	12,800	Equity capital	7,800
		Total capital	12,800

During the year the following year the firm bought £50,000 worth of goods. It paid for £47,500 of this and also for the £3,500 owed at the start of the year. Not all the goods were sold and the value of goods in stock at the end of the year was £6,500.

The firm also paid out £80,800 in other expenses and paid the tax due. In addition a van was bought for £12,000. The total depreciation charge for the year worked out at £3,200.

Sales during the year were £140,000, most of which was paid for with cash, except for one invoice for £6,000 which was unpaid at the end. The debtors of £1,300 all paid up what they owed. It was decided that a dividend of £3,000 would be paid next year on this year's results.

Here is the profit and loss account for the year:

EXAMPLE

Cashly and Company Ltd
Profit and loss account
Year ended 31 December 1991

		£
Sales		140,000
Opening stock	2,500	
Purchases	50,000	
	52,500	
Less: closing stock	6,500	
Cost of sales	46,000	
Other costs	80,800	
Depreciation	3,200	
Total costs		130,000
Operating profit		10,000
Taxation		2,500
Net profit after tax		7,500
Dividends		3,000
Retained earnings		4,500

Here is the year-end balance sheet:

EXAMPLE

Cashly and Company Ltd
Balance sheet at 31st December 1991

Assets	£	Capital	£
Fixed assets	12,800	Trade creditors	2,500
Stocks	6,500	Taxation	2,500
		Dividends	3,000
Debtors	6,000	Bank overdraft	5,000
Cash	–	Current liabilities	13,000
Total assets	25,300	Equity capital	12,300
		Total capital	25,300

There are two ways of looking at the cash flow of the firm.
The first is the 'In and Out' method:

EXAMPLE

	£
Cash in from sales	140,000
Less debtors at end:	6,000
Plus last year's debtors paid up	1,300
Net sales receipts	135,000
Outgoings:	
Last year's bills (creditors)	3,500
This year's purchases of goods	47,500
Other expenses	80,800
Van cost	12,000

Tax	1,500
Total outgoings	145,300
Balance for year (net cash outflow)	−10,000
Starting cash	5,000
Ending overdraft	5,000

The second is similar to the statement found in most companies' accounts nowadays – the cash-flow statement:

EXAMPLE

	£
Inflows:	
Operating profit	10,000
+ Depreciation	3,200
Operating inflows	13,200
Outflows from operations:	
Increase in stocks	4,000
Increase in debtors	4,700
Decrease in creditors	1,000
Increase in working capital	9,700
Net inflow from operations	3,500
Other outflows:	
Taxation	1,500
Purchase of fixed assets	12,000
	13,500
Net inflow (outflow)* in the year	(10,000)

Opening cash	5,000
Less: outflow in the year	−10,000
Cash (overdraft)* at year end	(5,000)

*This way of presenting the information (using brackets) is a common accounting convention where the answer may be positive or negative. Normally the brackets indicate negative (or the opposite of the other items in a list of statistics).

A little study of these figures will be rewarding, because the cash-flow statement makes it possible to connect the balance sheet and the profit and loss account and satisfactorily explains why the cash in the two balance sheets has changed so much, even though a reasonable profit was earned. Certainly, when looking at the published accounts of firms, you should never ignore the cash flow. A useful aid is to mark each item 'In' or 'Out', so that it will be very easy to spot what has happened to the firm's money.

SUMMARY OF THE CHAPTER

■ The three accounting statements of the balance sheet, the profit and loss account and the cash flow are drawn up for every business enterprise and all need to be read as aspects of the same story.

■ The layout will differ from firm to firm and from country to country, but the contents are essentially the same, and often they are the only source of data available to us about a company.

Something to do: write off to well-known companies (the Public Relations department, usually) and ask to be sent a copy of their latest report and accounts. It costs you the price of a stamp and will enable you to look at specific examples of their layout and content.

7 *Budgetary control*

Most managers have to work to a budget. More often than not they have to prepare budgets, and then actual results are compared with the budget as a means of exercising control. In this chapter we shall set out the features of budgets and describe the difference between 'good' and 'bad' budgets.

WHAT IS A BUDGET?

A budget is a statement which expresses somebody's plans in quantitative, usually monetary, terms. For example, a sales manager may say, 'Next year I am going to put ten men on the road and they are going to bring in a lot of money for the firm.' That is his plan, but a budget will go further than that and actually identify the following things:

- How much money are the salesmen going to bring in?
- When will the sales actually be made?
- How much will the salesmen cost the firm in terms of salaries, commission, travelling expenses, entertaining customers, etc?

If it is properly set up, the purpose of the budget is to give the manager the chance to determine for himself precisely how the part of the organisation for which he is responsible will fare. It will also give his own boss the opportunity to make sure that the proposals are in line with the overall strategic plans of the firm. Finally a budget is useful for the financial people within an organisation; it enables them to plan how much money to borrow or invest at different times of the year. Individual departmental budgets, therefore, form the basis by which total operating and financial plans can be made, as well as providing individual managers with a measure of their own performance.

Budgets are to be found in most organisations, both in the public and business sector, except the very small and the very inefficient. Indeed, many individuals create budgets themselves for their own private affairs by estimating income and expenditure: balancing expenditure month by month so that the amount of money in the bank never falls beyond a certain level (which may not necessarily be zero!). A budget, therefore, is the plan turned into numbers.

BUDGETARY CONTROL

Budgetary control is the name given to the control system which uses budgets as the basis for monitoring actual performance. If the budgetary control function knows precisely what is required, then it can set up the appropriate system to capture the figures and present them in the most suitable way.

Key elements of a good control system

1   There must be a plan. This may be expressed as a target, as a standard or as some other statement of what is wanted. However expressed, it must be capable of being compared with what is actually happening.

2   There must be a comparison between planned performance and what is actually happening. This is usually called *monitoring performance.* With cost control systems, the accounting information in the budget must be defined and presented in exactly the same way as the information in the 'actual' accounts.

3   The comparison must be made often. This ensures that any variations between planned performance and actual events are identified before serious adverse effects occur. In some situations it may only be necessary to make the comparison monthly. In others continuous monitoring may be advisable.

4   Variances must be reported to the responsible manager. This is often referred to as the *feedback loop.* All significant variances have to be fed back to whoever can take action to

sort out the problem. Note the key phrase 'significant variances'. There is little point in wasting a manager's time telling him the sales force expenses amounted to £5,001 last week compared with a budget of £5,000. The difference is insignificant. If, however, the expenses had actually turned out to be £5,200 then the manager concerned must be told what has happened.

5   Feedback must be fast. If there is a significant variance, the quicker the fact is reported to the manager concerned the quicker something can be done to solve the difficulty. The longer the period of time between the event and the reporting, the greater the likelihood of a disaster.

6   A decision has to be taken. Faced with a significant variance in performance, the wise manager will choose a suitable course of action. How quickly he does this will depend on the nature of the difficulty; some things can be dealt with instantly, other problems can best be solved if a little time is taken to think them through and discuss them with colleagues. There are only three possible courses of action:

    – Do nothing at all. This is only recommended if the reason for the problem is a unique occurrence and is unlikely to happen again.
    – Change the plan. Events occur outside the control of anyone in the organisation. If, for instance, the buyers are working on a target price for a particular raw material of £100 a kilo and a revolution in the country where the material comes from puts the price up to £150 a kilo, in that situation alternative plans have to be made.
    – Adjust operations. The problem may have arisen because part of the organisation is not working at a normal level of efficiency. The manager must quickly identify the underlying cause of the problem, then take steps to cure it.

7   Good news or bad news? Often an adverse variance is used as a way of criticising a manager's performance. This may well be needed on occasions, but a better use is as a basis for a discussion on how things can be improved. On the other hand, if the variance is favourable (or if there is no variance at all), too often nothing is said or done by way of recognition. When things are going according to plan, it is worth informing the people responsible of the good news. This does three things: it

stops them worrying, it helps them resist the temptation to meddle and they feel good.

8   The costs of the system must be justifiable. The control systems in a jumbo jet are justified not just because the machine is very expensive, but also because life is involved. With cost control systems, the potential loss involved should greatly exceed the cost of running the system.

Other budgetary control matters

Identifying the responsible manager

Everything that happens in a company is the responsibility of someone, and every item of cost must be controlled by a manager. The manager with the budget and the responsibility must also have the power and authority to do something if things go adrift. Ultimately, in every organisation, the chief officer receives the overall variance on the budgeted profit and loss account. This is not to say that he should see every detail and personally account for every penny of variation. He has to account for the overall result, but subordinates have to account to him for their own spheres of responsibility. It is simply effective delegation.

Is an adverse variance always bad?

The short answer is 'No', because sometimes additional costs are incurred in making extra sales. A poorly developed budgetary control system will not allow for this, so to be sure that proper account is taken, the report that accompanies the variance statement must state:

■ what happened;
■ precisely where the variances occurred.

False budgets for added protection

If a manager is asked to prepare a budget for his department he can start with a blank piece of paper and calculate what he needs in order to be able to perform his duties satisfactorily (sometimes known as *zero-based budgeting*). Or he can work on the basis of previous years' figures, adding a percentage to cover inflation and growth in the volume of work to be done.

If, however, the budget is an expenses-only budget and considered in isolation by a vetting committee, the manager may well decide to add on an extra 20 per cent to the total cost, because previous experience indicates that the committee will prime the budget anyway.

This kind of activity is not uncommon and gives budgetary control a bad name. It is found most frequently in organisations which do not really understand the nature of the technique, and where the committee is more concerned to make sure the budgets add up to a reasonable-looking figure, rather than representing real plans in realistic monetary terms.

The activity is also to be found where overall expenditure limits have been set and the sum of individuals' budgets exceeds the total. This occurs frequently in government departments and local authorities when it is felt that taxes cannot be raised high enough to meet spending departments' demands. Similarly, in business, capital expenditure is sometimes 'rationed' if insufficient finance is available to satisfy all needs.

Padding the budget

Sometimes budgets are set artificially high, if the manager knows that he will be judged on the size of the variance – if the actual costs of his department are much less than the budget, he gets a pat on the back. Clearly this is not a desirable system.

The imposed budget

Another way of setting budgets is if someone other than the responsible manager does it. So, instead of saying to the manager, 'What are your spending intentions next year?' the question becomes a statement: 'This is what you are entitled to spend next year.' If the manager is lucky he gets more than he needs, but if he receives less than he needs he may be forced to make cuts that will harm his department's efficiency or effectiveness.

Inflexible budgetary control

In large organisations it is not uncommon to hear people say, 'We cannot go to the lavatory unless it is in the budget', and 'The system is so tight it is strangling initiative.' Budgetary control can be a very effective system. It must, however, have flexibility; otherwise initiative is lost. Eventually the system runs the organisation and that can be fatal.

ESSENTIAL FEATURES OF BUDGETARY CONTROL

The system must:

- have the support of top management;
- be in tune with long-term aims, objectives and strategies;
- be prepared early;
- involve every level of responsibility;
- be flexible;
- be understood and appreciated by all users; and
- have each part corresponding with the responsibility of each manager.

SUMMARY OF CHAPTER

- Budgets are essential in all organisations. Properly used they describe in monetary terms the plans for the coming year or years.
- Also they are used to ensure that events are turning out the way they were planned and that any problems can be nipped in the bud. Too often, though, budgets are misused, too slowly produced, forced on people and unhelpful.

EXERCISE

What about your own budgets, both domestically and at work?

Do you have them?

Do you use them?

Do they enable you to control financial matters?

If your budgets echo any of the problems outlined in this chapter, or if they fall short of the ideals, then what are you going to do about it?

8 Costs and costing

In this chapter we are going to look at ways of answering two questions that are often asked in business, namely:

- How much do our products, services or jobs cost us?
- Do we make any money out of them?

If we go into a shop and buy a tin of paint for £2.00 it is easy to work out the cost. Similarly, firms buying in goods or materials can easily determine how much an article costs.

The problem arises if some value is added to the original item and if more than one item (which may be a product or a service) is involved. A complex piece of equipment may have dozens of component parts and may be worked on by many different people with different skills, as well as being shipped out to a customer along with many other items.

EXERCISE: A COSTING PROBLEM

Joe buys and sells two sizes of a product:

Product A he buys for £5.00
Product B he buys for £8.00

He has overheads amounting to £30,000 in the year (rent, rates, wages, advertising etc.) and he expects to sell 10,000 of Product A and 20,000 of Product B. He thinks he can charge £6.50 for A and £10.00 for B. He does not think there is any scope for an increase in either of these prices without affecting demand significantly, but he thinks sales could be higher if prices were lower.

Do you think that his prices are sensible?

Will he make any money?

If so, which product is doing the best?

The presentation of the relevant accounting information would look like this, using the 'normal' trading account format:

EXAMPLE

Joe's Trading Company Ltd
Forecast trading account
January 1999

		£
Sales: A 10,000 @ 6.50		65,000
B 20,000 @ 10.00		200,000
Total sales		265,000
Less cost of sales:		
A 10,000 @ 5.00	50,000	
B 20,000 @ 8.00	160,000	
Total cost of sales		210,000
Total gross profit		55,000
Less overheads		30,000
Trading profit		25,000

So from these figures it is possible to deduce that Joe will make a reasonable profit if he succeeds in selling the quantity of goods estimated, in total. However, it is not clear which of the two products is helping most, nor if more profit would be made by reducing prices and selling more.

To help us decide, an alternative way of showing this information would be in a form more usually found in management accounting statements:

EXAMPLE

	Product A (£)	Product B (£)
Selling price	6.50	10.00
Cost price	5.00	8.00
Gross profit per unit	1.50	2.00
Expected sales	10,000	20,000
Total gross profit	15,000	40,000

At this point, the gross profit for each of the two products can be seen clearly. Sometimes this figure is referred to as the 'contribution' and it is not difficult to calculate what the gross profit, or contribution, would be with different prices and different sales volumes:

EXERCISE

Product A

What is the gross profit for this product if:

1. Selling price is £6.25 and sales are 11,500?

2. Selling price is £6.00 and sales are 13,000?

> 3. Selling price is £5.95 and sales are 14,000?
>
> 4. Selling price is £5.50 and sales are 16,000?

The gross profit in each situation can be shown like this:

EXAMPLE

	Option 1 (£)	Option 2 (£)	Option 3 (£)	Option 4 (£)
Price	6.25	6.00	5.95	5.50
Cost price	5.00	5.00	5.00	5.00
Gross profit	1.25	1.00	0.95	0.50
Volume sold	11,500	13,000	14,000	16,000
Total gross profit	14,375	13,000	13,300	8,000

The conclusion is easy to see; none of these options provide more gross profit than the original price and volume equation, although sales volume would be considerable higher. If the aim of the exercise was just to capture market share, then the very low price would be the best – but what a price to have to pay! The next chapter looks a little more closely at pricing problems.

ALLOCATING OVERHEADS

What about the overheads? So far, the overheads of the business have been ignored. The focus has been on the gross profit of the business, but it can be argued that the overheads have to be brought into the calculations. If they are, we immediately run into another difficulty – how to divide the overheads between the two products.

EXERCISE

> How many ways of splitting up the £30,000 in Joe's Trading
> Company can you think of?

Here are three simple ways of dividing up the overheads, although
in practice many methods are used and sometimes different
formulae are applied to different overhead items:

EXAMPLE

1. 50:50, so each product bears an overhead of £15,000. This
   would be equal to:

   £1.50 a unit for Product A
   £0.75 a unit for Product B.

		£
2.	In relation to the volume sold:	
	Product A sales volume	10,000
	Product B sales volume	20,000
	Total sales volume	30,000
	Total overheads	30,000
	Overheads per unit (both products)	1.00
	Product A's overheads are, therefore:	10,000
	Product B's overheads are, therefore:	20,000
3.	In relation to sales value:	
	Product A sales value	65,000
	Product B sales value	200,000
	Total sales value	265,000
	Total overheads	30,000

Product A's overheads are, therefore: 7,358
(being 65/265ths of £30,000)

                                                  This is £0.74 a unit.

Product B's overheads are, therefore: £22,642
(being 200/265ths of £30,000).

                                                  This is £1.13 a unit.

The conclusion is:

The overhead cost a product bears depends entirely on the method of allocating the overheads between them.

FULL, OR TOTAL, ABSORPTION COSTING

If now we take off the overheads from the gross profit using each of the three formulae (nos. 1–3 in the following example), we get a notional profit figure for each product. This technique is called absorption costing, since all the overheads are absorbed by the products:

EXAMPLE

Product A Allocation method:	1 (£)	2 (£)	3 (£)
Gross profit as above	15,000	15,000	15,000
Less overheads	15,000	10,000	7,358
Notional profit	0	5,000	7,642
Profit per unit	0	0.50	0.76

Product B

Allocation method:	1	2	3
	(£)	(£)	(£)
Gross profit as above	40,000	40,000	40,000
Less overheads	15,000	20,000	22,642
Notional profit	25,000	20,000	17,358
Profit per unit	1.25	1.00	0.87

The total profit remains the same in all cases but each product shows a different level depending on the allocation basis. This can lead to problems. For example, what should we do about product A if the first basis of allocation is taken? It seems as though it is not making any money. So do we raise the price and hope that sales do not fall much? Or do we scrap the product? Or should we try to buy a cheaper version?

These may be fair questions to ask, but to assume that the product is not making a profit is erroneous thinking. The message is:

Products do not make profits; they contribute *to the overheads and the profit of the firm.*

Notice the stress on the word 'contribute': contribution is a very important concept.

THE RECOVERY PROBLEM

Full absorption costing can be used in management accounts for reporting purposes. Every time a unit of product is sold, a portion of the overheads is 'recovered'. For example, if the basis of allocation was by volume (Method 2 above), then every unit sold of product A makes a profit of £0.50, and recovers £1.00 of overheads. Product B makes a profit of £1.00 and recovers £1.00 of overheads as well.

Often these figures are used to test whether the firm is up to budget, but complications soon arise if volumes do not turn out the way they were planned.

Study the simple set of accounts below and try to identify the problem:

EXAMPLE

Joe's Trading Company Ltd
Trading account report
January 1999

	Budget (£)	Actual (£)
Sales volume: A	10,000	8,600
B	20,000	18,000
Sales value: A	65,000	55,900
B	200,000	180,000
Total sales	265,000	235,900
Gross profit: A @ £1.50	15,000	12,900
B @ £2.00	40,000	36,000
Total gross profit	55,000	48,900
Less Overheads: A @ £1.00	−10,000	−8,600
B @ £1.00	−20,000	−18,000
Trading profit	£25,000	£22,300

Note: the same 'actual' profit figure can be deduced by using the 'profit per unit' figures for both lines:

A sales 8,600 @ £0.50	£4,300
B sales 18,000 @ £1.00	£18,000
Total profit	£22,300

If this situation arose, where sales failed to match budget, it is said that there was an 'under-recovery of overheads'. The total recovered was £26,600 (i.e. £8,600 + £18,000) − £3,400 less than budget – and if £30,000 was actually spent on overheads then the profit figure of £22,300 is wrong!

- The actual gross profit is correct: £48,900
- But the overheads are: £30,000
- Actual profit is: £18,900

What happened? The overhead recovery rate only applies if the actual volume sold is exactly the same as the budget. Here actual sales are lower, therefore the recovery rate should be £1.13 a unit (approximately).

This example should alert you to the dangers of costing. Be very careful in interpreting such information.

Two definitions

- Marginal costing analyses costs as far as gross profit only.
- Total absorption costing allocates overheads to products to arrive at a notional profit for each.

Note: although the above discussion relates to products, the concepts apply equally to firms which provide a range of services – holiday firms can cost a holiday marginally or on an absorption basis, for instance.

Problems of marginal costing include the danger of allowing products to survive 'at the margin', reducing the firm's overall profits (it is possible to end up selling masses of products, each making a contribution, but making no profit at all). Also, pricing new products may not be as effective (especially if there is no 'market price' for the item) if no account is taken of overheads, especially as the additional product may cause overheads to rise. An example of this is when an extra van is needed to distribute the new line to customers.

Problems of absorption costing are that it is cumbersome, especially in very complex companies, with many products and locations; all allocation methods are arbitrary to a greater or lesser degree – it is not scientific – so the conclusion may be misleading; moreover, every time the volume sold changes, or a new line is introduced, or costs change, all the sums have to be recalculated.

The key questions in costing
- Can we make more profit as a whole by changing the price of the product?
- If we drop the product does the company as a whole make more profit?
- If we introduce a new line will the business as a whole make more profit?

JOB COSTING

A particular type of costing problem arises where a job is being carried out. Garage workshops, plumbers, builders, printers and maintenance engineers are among the types of trade where success at costing is vital. Consider this situation:

EXAMPLE: ERNIE'S PLUMBING SERVICES LTD

Ernie employs four fully qualified plumbers and operates out of an office with a small store and workshop at the back. Each plumber has a van, and Ernie advertises his services in the local papers. As requests come in, his assistant logs the call and directs one of the plumbers to the customer, having first given the caller an idea of the cost.

Ernie is reviewing his prices for next year. Here are the facts:

	£
Total wages, pensions and national insurance	86,000
Rent, rates	16,000
Electricity, gas, water	1,900
Telephone, post etc.	4,800
Advertising	10,000
Van costs (including depreciation)	33,000
Other costs	28,300
Total forecast expenditure for year	180,000

Ernie anticipates that the total hours available for working on jobs will be 1,800 per plumber. This allows for holidays, sickness and lunches, but includes driving time and some unproductive time as well. The total available hours are therefore 7,200.

The price of a job depends on the time it takes, so Ernie has calculated that he needs to charge £25.00 an hour to cover his costs. To make a profit he needs to charge more, so he adds 20 per cent to the rate and arrives at a charge-out rate of £30.00 an hour. He might make this the minimum call-out charge, too.

As long as he 'sells' an average of 600 hours a month at £30.00 an hour, he will cover his costs and make a profit of £3,000. (His sales would be £18,000 and his costs 1/12th of £180,000 i.e. £15,000, giving a trading profit of £3,000.)

EXERCISE

> Work out the consequences if in the first three months of trading, he manages to sell only 1,500 hours of service and all his costs amount to £54,000.

There would be a shortfall of £9,000 as a result of selling insufficient hours:

Sales 1,500 hours at £30.00	£45,000
Overheads	£54,000
Trading loss	£9,000

This is instead of a profit of £9,000. What would you do if you were Ernie?

You have three options:

1   Do nothing and hope that sales will be better than budget for the rest of the year. That is, accept the loss.
2   Cut your costs for the rest of the year.
3   Revise your recovery rate.

Option no. 3 has curious consequences. Work out what Ernie would have to charge for the rest of the year to achieve his original budgeted profit. Here are the facts:

Overhead costs as planned for 9 months	£135,000
Overheads under-recovered so far	£9,000
Total hours now available	5,400
Desired profit for the year	£36,000

He would have to sell all the remaining hours at £33.33 to achieve a profit of £36,000. His problem is that some customers may desert him at these rates and so he would lose even more money. So then he puts his rates up even higher, and even fewer sales are made, and so on.

The lesson from this example is:

Charge-out rates should preferably be set annually, with regard to market conditions, as well as expected costs.

SUMMARY OF THE CHAPTER

- Costing products, services and jobs is not a simple task, and the unwary can easily draw wrong conclusions and make poor decisions.
- Marginal costing, with its emphasis on *contribution*, is easy to use, especially in complex process industries.
- Absorption costing makes everyone aware of overheads and can help in questions of pricing. It can be complex and time-consuming if handled inexpertly.
- Always be sure to establish at the start what you want to find out and always be sure to discover the effect of a change on the profits of the firm as a whole.

9 *Break-even analysis*

This chapter looks at the nature of costs and how an understanding of their nature can help in planning the price, volume and profit equation.

HOW COSTS BEHAVE

Some costs tend to remain unaffected by variations in the amount of business carried out by the company. A good example is the rent of a warehouse. It is of no consequence whether the place operates twenty–four hours a day, seven days a week, or whether it opens only on Saturdays. The rental charge to the firm will be exactly the same. This type of cost is sometimes called a *fixed cost*; within a period of a few months the cost will not change as volume varies. If, eventually, sales drop to a very low level, the firm may decide to move into smaller, cheaper premises. In this case there would be a new fixed cost for a while. Similarly, if sales rose rapidly a new warehouse would be needed, costing more. There would be another new fixed cost. In the long run, no costs are really 'fixed'.

In contrast, some costs vary directly with the volume of business carried out. The obvious examples of this are the commissions paid to salesmen, fuel costs of delivery vehicles and the cost of goods or materials used by the firm in its processes, or just sold on. These costs are called *variable costs.*

Often fixed costs are more or less the same as the overheads of the company, whereas variable costs often equate to the 'cost of sales' figure used in the calculation of gross profit.

Here is an example of the way the costs of a company can be split:

EXAMPLE: THE SUPER COFFEE COMPANY

The owners buy coffee beans in bulk at £9 a kilo, and pack them into small bags (adding a packaging cost of £1 a kilo). The variable cost is therefore £10 a kilo. They sell it for £15 a kilo.

Next year their budgeted expenses and overheads, including staff costs, rent, rates and advertising will amount to £175,000. These costs they believe to be fixed, because the staff are mainly themselves and family – the only outsiders being close family friends. Their small advertising budget is already firmly committed. They believe, on the basis of experience, that they will sell about 40,000 kilos in the year.

How much profit will they make if this actually happens and costs work out exactly as planned?

Their budgeted trading account would look like this:

The Super Coffee Company
Budget trading account

	£
Sales: 40,000 kilos @ £15.00	600,000
Cost of sales: 40,000 kilos @ 10.00	400,000
Gross profit	200,000
Fixed costs	175,000
Trading profit	25,000

Another way of showing this situation is:

	£
Gross profit per kilo	5.00
Volume to be sold	40,000
Total gross profit	200,000
Less: fixed costs	175,000
Trading profit	25,000

What would happen to the trading profit if the volume sold fell to only 38,000 kilos?

The trading account would look like this:

	£
Gross profit per kilo	5.00
Volume to be sold in kilos	38,000
Total gross profit	190,000
Less: fixed costs	175,000
Trading profit	15,000

It is easy to see that the drop in profits (from £25,000 to £15,000) is much greater, relatively, than the drop in the volume sold (from 40,000 to 38,000).

What would happen to the trading profit if the volume sold fell to only 35,000 kilos?

The trading account would now look like this:

	£
Gross profit per kilo	5.00
Volume to be sold in kilos	35,000
Total gross profit	175,000
Less: fixed costs	175,000
Trading profit	---

The problem for the firm now is that its volume is sufficient only to cover the fixed costs of the business. Any further drop in volume would result in a loss.

In this example it can be said that the volume of 35,000 kilos is the *break-even* volume. The concept is important to all business operations, since it clearly shows that a considerable volume of sales has to be made before a profit is made. In other words, no trading profit is made until sufficient gross profit has been generated to pay for the fixed costs of the business.

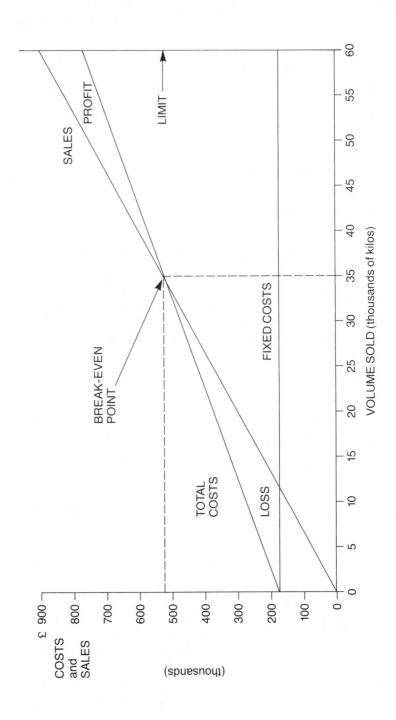

The concept can be portrayed graphically, as shown. The sales line starts at zero and the total costs line at £175,000 – the expected sum of fixed costs for the year. For a while total costs exceed sales – and a loss is made. At the break-even point, where the two lines cross, the firm starts to make a profit. However, its ability to make a profit is limited by the capacity of its fixed costs – beyond a certain volume they could not cope, so a limit has been drawn to show the maximum that could be made, given those fixed costs. To sell more, the firm would have to incur more fixed costs.

A FORMULA FOR BREAK-EVEN

Most companies do not have a single product like the one in our above example. Either a variey of products are sold with different prices and margins, or a service is being sold with no easily identifiable sales 'unit'. In this case a simple formula can be used to find out what sales are needed in, £ terms, to make a profit. This is:

Fixed costs divided by gross profit percentage multiplied by 100

Using the Super Coffee Company example above:

EXAMPLE

Fixed costs	£175,000
Divided by: gross profit margin	
($£15 - £10 = £5/£15 \times 100$)	33.33%
Equals:	5,250
Multiplied by 100 equals:	£525,000

So sales to the value of £525,000 have to be made before any profit is earned. This is 35,000 kilos at £15 a kilo. Until the break-even point is reached, all the sales are contributing to the overheads (or fixed costs of the firm); in other words, a loss is still being made.

SUMMARY OF THE CHAPTER

■ The idea of a break-even point is simple, namely that profit is not earned until all the fixed costs have been paid for out of gross profits.

■ In the long run all fixed costs must be capable of reduction – or even elimination – but within the timespan of a few months this is impossible. It is very important, therefore, that everyone knows just how much has to be sold before profit is made.

10 *Capital investment appraisal*

Here is a business proposition for you to consider:

Spend £40,000 on a special machine which can convert old newspapers into fine quality writing paper and you will make a cash profit (before depreciation but after tax) of £16,000 a year straight off. The machine will be valueless after four years.

Would you go for it? (Assume that it is not a problem finding the money.)

You may well argue that you do not have enough information to enable a sensible decision to be made. The 'facts' you would ask for would certainly include:

■ How has the profit figure been calculated?
■ Where did the sales and cost estimates come from – and how reliable are they?

Once you are happy that the costings themselves are reasonable, the first step is to establish if the project would generate an adequate return on the money invested. A simple calculation is:

Profit after tax divided by capital invested

The profit after depreciation would be £6,000, because there would be an annual depreciation charge of £10,000 to deduct from the cash profit of £16,000 (i.e. £40,000 capital cost spread over four years). Or:

£6,000/£40,000 = 15% = the return on capital employed

This is better than putting the money in the bank. But what happens if the machine has an expected life of only two years and is then scrapped? Is the return still 15 per cent? Clearly not, because most of the investment would have been lost. The success of the venture depends on the length of time the machine will operate, producing goods for which there is likely to be a demand. If the project lasts only two years, then the depreciation would have to be £20,000 a year – resulting in a loss of £4,000 a year instead of the £6,000 profit.

Therefore in all capital investment decisions the *expected life* of the project has to be taken into consideration in assessing capital investment proposals and there are three main approaches:

- ■ average return on capital;
- ■ payback period;
- ■ discounted rate of return.

AVERAGE RATE OF RETURN METHOD

Suppose we guess that the machine will last five years and will then have to be scrapped as worthless and that the profit before depreciation is £16,000 a year for each of the five years. The average return on investment is calculated as follows.

EXAMPLE

	£
Annual profit before depreciation	16,000
Less: depreciation (one-fifth of £40,000)	8,000
Profit after depreciation	8,000
Total profit £8,000 p.a. × 5 years	40,000
Average annual profit is	8,000
Investment was	40,000
So the average return is	20%

What would happen to the return if the project was expected to last eight years?

Depreciation would be £5,000 a year (one-eighth of £40,000), resulting in a profit after tax of £11,000.

EXERCISE

Fill in the figures for yourself:

Profit £_____ p.a. for 8 years =	£_____
Average annual profit is	£_____
Investment was	£40,000
So the average return is	_____%

Does the project look so appealing now?

You should have a return of 27.5 per cent on the project.

EXERCISE

Now try to calculate the return where the profits vary from year to year. In this case the project is also over eight years and the annual depreciation charge is therefore £5,000.

Here are the profit figures (bracketed figures indicate a loss):

	Year 1	(£1,700)
	Year 2	£4,100
	Year 3	£7,800
	Year 4	£9,800
	Year 5	£13,100
	Year 6	£15,000
	Year 7	£18,500
	Year 8	£21,400
Total profit		£_____
Average annual profit		£_____
Total amount invested		£40,000
Average return on capital invested		__%

The result of these calculations is 27.5 per cent. (The total profit is £88,000, giving an annual average of £11,000. This is 27.5 per cent of £40,000.) It appears that the project is just as profitable as the one where profits every year are £11,000 consistently.

Note: a variation on this method is to take the average capital employed. This doubles the returns in each case.

PAYBACK PERIOD METHOD

This method answers the question: how quickly do we get our money back?

In the last example, an investment of £40,000 produced profits amounting to £88,000 over an eight-year period, though the profits were different each year. However, the return was the same as for the project where the profits amounted to the *same* sum each year. Thus the method ignores the way the money flows into the company and it seems reasonable to suppose that in reality the timing of the inflows makes some difference.

The profits were arrived at by deducting depreciation of £5,000 a year. So if this sum is added back, we get the *cash flows* for each year for the two projects, thus:

EXAMPLE

	Project A (£)	Project B (£)
Year 1	16,000	3,300
Year 2	16,000	9,100
Year 3	16,000	12,800
Year 4	16,000	14,800
Year 5	16,000	18,100
Year 6	16,000	20,000
Year 7	16,000	23,500
Year 8	16,000	26,400
Total cash flow	128,000	128,000

If these figures represent the cash flowing into the business each year, it is easy to see that the outlay of £40,000 will be recovered in just two and a half years in the case of Project A, but Project B would have a *payback period* of four years. Therefore if only one of these projects could be financed, it would seem sensible to go for the one which pays back soonest. Some business people would consider this to be a reasonable proposition, arguing that because of the risks inherent in long-term projects, the sooner you get the money back the better.

DISCOUNTED RATE OF RETURN

The weakness of the payback method is that cash flows after the project has paid for itself are ignored and can, therefore, lead to a really good long-term project being turned down. Here is a simple example of the danger:

EXAMPLE

	Project X (£000)	Project Z (£000)
Cost	60	60
Cash flow: Year 1	5	30
2	10	30
3	15	10
4	30	10
5	40	10
6	40	–
7	40	–

Project X pays for itself in four years, but Project Z in only two. Project X however generates far more cash later. Its average return is much higher, but the weakness of the average rate of return system is that it ignores how quickly the money comes back.

Discounted cash flow (DCF) techniques aim to overcome the drawbacks of the other two methods. The basic concept is simple:

Money has a 'time value'.

If I invest £100 today and receive back £121 two years from now, it is not difficult to see that the money will have been invested at an interest rate of 10 per cent per annum, compounded. (i.e. after one year, interest of £10 will be added to the £100, making £110. In year two, 10 per cent is earned on £110 – an extra £11, making £121 in total.) It can be said that the *present value* of £121, in two years' time at 10 per cent, is £100. In other words, £121 in two years' time, discounted at 10 per cent, has a present value of £100.

With business capital projects the actual percentage return is usually difficult to calculate and the technique used, based on discounting, is called the *internal rate of return* (IRR) or the 'true' rate of return.

To calculate the present value of a sum of money in the future, instead of going through the compound interest calculations as described above, a *discount rate* is used instead. In the above example this is:

$$\frac{£100}{£121} = 0.826$$

This is the present value factor at 10 per cent for two years.
The data are usually presented in the following manner:

EXAMPLE

Year	*Annual cash flow* $£$	×	*PV factor @10.0%*	=	*Present value* $£$
0	−100		1.000		−100
1	0		0.909		0
2	+121		0.826		100
	Net present value (NPV)				0

A present value (PV) factor at every rate of interest, and for any
number of years, can be calculated in this way. Luckily, the data
are available in the form of discount tables and most computers
can do the calculations virtually automatically. The *net present
value* is zero in this case. If the interest rate chosen for discounting
had been incorrect, then the net present value would not have
been zero, as shown in the following calculations:

EXAMPLE

Year	Annual cash flow ×	PV factor @14.0% =	Present value
	£		£
0	−100	1.000	−100
1	0	0.877	0
2	+121	0.769	93
	Net present value (NPV)		−£7

This tells us that the real rate of return is less than 14 per cent. (We would only need to invest £93 for two years at 14 per cent to realise £121.)

If the interest rate chosen had been too low, the figures might be like this:

EXAMPLE

Year	Annual cash flow ×	PV factor @8.0% =	Present value
	£		£
0	−100	1.000	−100
1	0	0.926	0
2	+121	0.857	104
	Net present value (NPV)		£4

This tells us that the real rate of return is more than 8 per cent. (We would need to invest £104 for two years at 8 per cent to realise £121.)

Imagine you are offered an investment opportunity, guaranteeing a sum of money in X years' time for a given investment now. To get at the real rate of return, instead of working out the compound interest rate, just apply PV factors for a few different interest rates. This will give you a good idea of the real merits of the offer.

Looking back at projects X and Z above (page 70) we can apply discount rates to each one and work out the real rate of return for each:

EXAMPLE

Project X

Year	Annual cash flow $\times$	PV @ 26.1% $=$	Present value
	£000		£000
0	−60	1.000	−60.0
1	+ 5	0.793	4.0
2	+10	0.629	6.3
3	+15	0.499	7.5
4	+30	0.396	11.9
5	+40	0.313	12.5
6	+40	0.249	9.9
7	+40	0.197	7.9
	Net present value		−

Note: all the numbers have been rounded off for simplification.

Project X has a real rate of return of 26.1 per cent. The rate of interest was . found by guesswork initially, and (without a computer) several attempts would have been made before the exact interest rate was found. Project Z, in contrast, shows a return of 20.5 per cent (the workings for this are not shown).

In this case, the decision to go ahead with the projects will depend on whether the return offered on them is better than the firm's minimum acceptable rate (the 'hurdle rate'). If the firm has a minimum rate of 18 per cent, then Project Z might be a bit too close for comfort, so Project X would be chosen. However, it could be argued that it takes much longer to earn 'decent' cash flows and there are greater risks involved.

There are critics of the IRR approach, not only because of the trial-and-error, time-consuming calculations. Oddities crop up occasionally: for instance if there are negative cash flows during the project's life, if there are varying interest rates over time, and in the case of assessing multiple projects.

A preferred technique is called the *net present value* method, and the procedure is:

1   Choose a minimum rate of return under which projects will be rejected.
2   Apply the appropriate present value factors to the cash flows.
3   Add the net present values.
4   If the net inflows exceed the initial outflow (i.e. the *net present value*), then accept the project.

EXAMPLE

Project Z
(Company minimum rate: 18%)

Year	Annual cash flow	×	PV @ 18.0%	=	Present value
	£000				£000
0	−60		1.000		−60.0
1	+30		0.847		25.4
2	+30		0.718		21.5
3	+10		0.609		6.1
4	+10		0.516		5.2
5	+10		0.437		4.4
		Net present value			+2.6

The project yields a return greater than 18 per cent and is therefore acceptable. If we were looking at several alternative uses for
our money, the projects with the greatest NPVs would be chosen
for implementation.

DEALING WITH INFLATION

Future cash flows can be calculated using prices and costs at
today's levels throughout the life of the project or can be 'inflated'
each year by an estimated increase in costs and prices. The effect
of inflating the numbers can be dramatic on the rate of return of a
project. For example, a project costing £60,000 and having a
seven-year life has an annual cash flow of £12,000. The DCF
return is 9.2 per cent. If the cash flow is increased by 5 per cent per
annum (so that in year 7 it amounts to £16,885) the DCF return
becomes nearly 14.7 per cent. Where the cash flows are increased
to account for inflation, the rate of interest used for discounting
must be the nominal rate of interest, not the real rate.

(If interest rates are at 12 per cent – the 'nominal rate' – and
inflation is 5 per cent, then the real rate of interest is 7 per cent.
This is the underlying cost of capital).

WHAT ABOUT THE ACCURACY OF THE FORECASTS?

Most forecasts are likely to be inaccurate to a greater or lesser
extent and the further off into the future the greater the probability
of error. To account for this uncertainty two techniques can be
built into capital investment projects which will help. They are:
sensitivity tests and *probability*, or *risk analysis.*

Sensitivity testing

The major assumptions about future cash flows relate to costs and
the volume of sales expected. These may vary considerably from
the 'best guess' used in the initial calculations. If it is thought at all
possible that the expected outcome may not occur, then two other
outcomes should be calculated:

■ the *best* likely outcome; and
■ the *worst* likely outcome.

Suppose Project Z, which we looked at on page 74, may generate 20 per cent less cash flow each year. Our NPV statement will look like this:

EXAMPLE

Project Z
(Company minimum rate: 18 per cent)

Year	Annual cash flow ×	PV @ 18.0% =	Present value
	£000		£000
0	−60	1.000	−60.0
1	+24	0.847	20.3
2	+24	0.718	17.2
3	+ 8	0.609	4.9
4	+ 8	0.516	4.1
5	+ 8	0.437	3.5
	Net present value		−10.0

In fact the IRR falls to a mere 8.4 per cent. If, in contrast, the cash flows could be 20 per cent higher, then the NPV will be +£15,100, giving an IRR of 32 per cent!

Management has to judge, before taking a decision, whether it is prepared to risk the possibility that the worst outcome may occur.

Risk analysis

With risk analysis, a view is taken as to the probability of certain events taking place. For instance with Project Z we may be fairly certain that the original cash flows will happen. Even so, there may be a small chance that the worst case could happen; we could have a disaster on our hands. By assigning a 'probability factor' to each possible outcome, we can judge the merits of the project, taking the odds into account.

So if there is:

- a 75 per cent probability of achieving 18 per cent, and
- a 15 per cent probability of achieving 8.4 per cent and
- a 10 per cent probability of achieving 32 per cent,

then on balance we may be prepared to go ahead. However, we should want to be very sure that if the worst happened we could still survive as a company.

DECISION TIME

All capital investment projects are concerned with future cash flows. The problem with the future is that it is uncertain, and all the techniques discussed in this chapter aim to reduce that uncertainty. They cannot, however, take away the difficulty of the decision; and the drawback is that if managers slavishly follow the formulae, do all the sums and base their decisions on these alone, the wrong decision may be taken. Managers have to exercise due diligence in their evaluation. They must use their expertise and commercial acumen and that of their colleagues. They must judge the 'fit' of the project to the rest of the business, and they must equally beware of being seduced by a glamorous-sounding opportunity, and of turning away a project just because it is not exciting. These things are what managers are paid for.

SUMMARY OF THE CHAPTER

- In dealing with capital investment projects, it is important to take account of the timing of the cash flows and the probability that one's estimates will be inaccurate.
- Discounting cash flows to present values gives a more realistic view of the returns on projects than straight arithmetical calculations, and must be carried out to test the viability of the project.
- Most of the mathematics can be easily handled by computer, but, as ever, the decision itself is the most important aspect and management must not abdicate this in favour of an automatic routine.

11 *Accounts analysis*

Whilst it is useful to be able to describe the contents of a company's accounts and to be able to say what the words mean, it is possible to get considerably more out of the accounts if you know how to analyse them.

One helpful approach to accounts analysis is to ask the question 'Should I invest my money in the company?' (this is assuming, of course, that you have some to invest), either to buy a small business for yourself or simply to purchase shares in an existing company. Before taking the decision, there are a number of questions you would need to ask. For instance:

■ Is the business making a profit?
■ How big is that profit?
■ Would I be able to make a reasonable living from it?
■ How much growth has there been over the last few years?

You don't buy a firm that is shrinking. This might lead to the question of prospects for the future – is it likely to grow?

Of course nobody can predict what will happen in the future, but a reasonable estimate has to be made. One other fundamental question to ask is how much the present owner wants for the business and how much goodwill is being demanded. A valuation of the assets would be included in the price. What exactly are the assets and are there a number of them or only a few?

If you were intent on buying your own business some of the other questions you might ask are:

■ Which products or services sell best?

■ Which are most profitable?
■ How many staff are employed and how much are they paid?
■ How much does the present owner take out of the business?
■ What is the rest of the money spent on?
■ Is this reasonable or excessive?
■ Does the business owe any money?
■ If so, to whom, and are the amounts reasonable?
■ Were there any debtors?
■ Was the debtor's figure reasonable?

It is also quite possible that you will need to borrow some money from the bank, either as working capital or to help pay for the business itself. In addition to all the questions you have asked already, the bank manager will also want to know:

■ How much interest could the firm pay?
■ If the business went broke, how would the bank get its money back?
■ How much would be a safe amount to lend?
■ What are the chances of the bank losing its money?
■ Is the present level of borrowing too high?

All these questions are bound to be asked by the bank manager – indeed, anyone lending money would be foolish not to ask them.

It will now be obvious that a number of questions should be asked before a business is bought or before money is lent to a business. Indeed, the same questions can be put even if the intention is merely to invest in a company, or simply to sell it. To sum up all of these in a sentence, it can be said that the aim of any such exercise is:

to take an investment decision, having considered the likely level of reward.

RISK AND REWARD

Risk can be defined as the possibility of ending up worse off than when you started. Reward is the expected return (or profit) you are likely to get back.

Consider these four very different ways of risking 'spare' money:

- Backing a horse at 100 to 1.
- Buying a stake in a company set up to look for gold in Central America.
- Buying some shares in British Gas.
- Putting the money on deposit in the bank.

It is not too difficult to see that the four options are ranked in descending order of riskiness, the horse race at the top of the list being a very risky proposition, whereas to put the money in the bank involves little risk (at least as far as a reputable British bank is concerned). If we turn to the question of potential reward, the four options have the same ranking – the horse could yield the best return (10,000 per cent in fifteen minutes). In contrast, the return on bank interest is very low. The general rule is this: that the highest returns go with the highest risk and the lowest returns tie in with the lowest risk.

The decision on which option to go for is a matter for individual taste, but the starting-point must always be the same, namely, *get the facts* – and with a company the facts are first revealed in the accounts. Do remember, however, that the accounts do not tell the whole story; other sources of information have to be used as well.

There are two kinds of facts in company accounts: the obvious and those which have to be uncovered. An obvious fact is one which answers the question directly. For example, in the list of questions that were posed on p. 79 some, like 'Were there any debtors?' and 'Did the business owe any money?', had obvious answers. These are easily obtained facts; but some of the questions were much trickier, such as 'Was the debtor's figure reasonable?' and 'Were the amounts owed by the firm reasonable?' If we want the facts in order to answer those questions we have to do a bit of digging – it's rather like a treasure hunt: some facts, some clues and then the search and a dig.

THE FOUR STEPS OF ANALYSIS

Step 1: Classify the questions

Group the questions into categories to start with, so that you can focus your attention on one aspect of the company at a time. The categories are these:

- Growth.
- Profitability (or returns).
- Financial strength (the bank's questions on p. 79).
- Assets.
- Borrowings (or financial structure).
- Operating efficiency.

All the questions on p. 79 can be fitted into these six categories, except that relating to the company's prospects.

Step 2: Treat the numbers

Drawing conclusions from untreated figures is a dangerous and difficult activity. So first reduce numbers to manageable size and then convert them to ratios. Reducing numbers to a manageable size is easy – simply round the numbers to three or four significant figures. Next, the numbers need to be turned to ratios. A ratio is a way of showing the size of a number relative to another number and the commonest type is a percentage. It describes a significant relationship and is essential for the next step of the hunt.

Step 3: Compare

The only sensible way of drawing a conclusion about a statistic is to use it to make a comparison. For instance, it is meaningless to say that a company has a profit margin of 8 per cent of sales unless that can be compared with the previous year, or with the competition.

Step 4: Draw your conclusions

The conclusion you will have arrived at after following this process will be much better than any views you might have had at the start.

KEY RATIOS FOR ANALYSIS

Now that we have considered the way to analyse accounts, the next job is to identify the key ratios which will actually help us to seek out the truth. The six categories of questions that we identified above will be looked at in turn.

CATEGORY 1: GROWTH

It is often best to start with the question: 'Has the company grown?' If the answer is 'No' or 'Not a lot', then the conclusion must be that there is some kind of problem, unless you know that the company has a policy of no growth. The simplest way to measure growth is to compare the volume sold in the first year with the volume sold in the second year, like this:

EXAMPLE

	Tons
Volume sold in 1993	2,600
Volume sold in 1992	2,000
Increase	600

Therefore the increase in tons sold is $(600/2,000) \times 100 = 30\%$

Volume is often very difficult to obtain in any sensible form; only if the item being compared is exactly the same from one year to another is the comparison valid.

The other obvious alternative to volume is to use turnover. This is always available but it is sometimes unduly affected by the cost of bought materials. In such cases it is helpful to use the value added figure, especially if the comparison you are going to make is against some general growth statistics – such as the growth of the economy as a whole.

Value added defined

Value added is the sum of:

Wages costs plus depreciation plus operating profit

and is equal to:

Sales revenues less the cost of all bought-in goods, components and services.

Other useful growth figures to calculate are:

■ Total assets.

- Equity capital (measuring the rate of growth of the company itself).
- Earnings.
- Physical items such as staff, operating units (e.g. lorries, branches, shops).

With growth figures it is helpful also to calculate the statistics for a four- or five-year period, because it is risky to look at only one year's growth rate.

CATEGORY 2: PROFITABILITY

It is not difficult for a company to make a profit. To make an adequate profit is harder, and to generate a more than satisfactory profit is fairly difficult (and fairly rare). It is easy to see whether a company has or has not made a profit, but it is not possible to tell by a quick glance at the accounts whether this profit is either adequate or satisfactory. Measures of profitability are designed to help us decide.

Several measures are in common use, so always check on the definition. The most commonly used numerators (i.e. the upper numbers of fractions) for the profitability ratio are:

- Operating profit.
- Earnings (profit after tax, before or after deducting extraordinary items).
- Dividends.

The most used denominators (i.e. the lower numbers of fractions) are:

- Assets employed (this can be total assets, or only operating assets, i.e. those used for trading purposes).
- Capital employed (total capital is the same as total assets). Often the term 'capital employed' refers to equity capital plus long-term liabilities.
- Equity capital.
- Number of issued shares.

Frequently the expression used to describe these ratios starts with the words 'return on ...' and so you will see:

- Return on assets (ROA). This is usually (operating profit / total assets) per cent.
- Return on capital employed (ROC or ROCE). If total capital is being used, the profit to refer to will be that before tax and interest payments. If equity capital is used, it is better to relate profit after tax to that. This is also called:
  - Return on equity (ROE).
  - Return on net assets (RONA).

You may also find the expression 'return on investment' (ROI) used. This is most often used in business planning to describe the profits that are expected from an investment and is calculated to see if the investment will be worthwhile.

All these ratios are trying to measure the same thing: namely how effectively the company has used the financial resources available to it during the year. Here are the relevant figures for three companies to illustrate the point:

EXAMPLE

Company	A (£000)	B (£000)	C (£000)
Operating profit	50	80	100
Less interest	10	–	40
	40	80	60
Less tax	20	40	30
Earnings	20	40	30
Total assets	500	400	400
Equity capital	400	300	100

Ratios:

	A	B	C
1 Operating profit / total assets %	10	20	25
2 Net profit after tax / equity capital %	5	13.3	30

Which asset and capital values to use

In calculating profitability ratios several different numbers can be used for the assets or capital part of the formula. It is traditional to compile the ratio by relating profit for the year to the value of capital in the balance sheet at the end of that year. However, in reality, profits are made by the assets or capital in use over the year as a whole, and therefore some kind of average should be used to get a better measure of profitability. Some writers consider that the asset values at the beginning of the year should be used for the denominator of the ratios, but there is not much support for this method. If you want to use an average instead, add the values at the start and the end of the year and then simply divide by two.

Other profitability measures

The ratios involving dividends and the amount of profit earned in relation to the shares themselves are of particular interest to shareholders. These ratios are earnings per share (EPS) and dividend ratios:

Earnings per share

There is an official definition for this contained in SSAP3:

profit after tax, after deducting minority interests and preference dividends, but before taking into account extraordinary items, divided by the number of equity shares at the date of the balance sheet entitled to dividends

This definition varies from country to country, and in Britain is under review by the Accounting Standards Board.

The answer is normally shown in Britain as a certain number of pence per share.

This ratio is much more popular in the USA than in Britain, where a company's progress each quarter is marked by the change in the EPS. However, it is difficult to get a good idea of a company's real progress in times of inflation since the earnings figure will be bigger, not because of efficiency but because of rising prices. Another limitation of EPS is that it cannot be used for comparing one company against another.

Dividend ratios

Three ratios involving dividends are important: per share, per cent and cover.

DIVIDEND PER SHARE   This is calculated by dividing the total dividends payable to shareholders in a year by the actual number of shares entitled to receive it. It is a quick way of seeing how a firm has been doing and is useful for investors since they can quickly work out how much dividend they will receive – assuming they know how many shares they have.

DIVIDEND PER CENT   This is simply the dividend per share divided by the nominal value of the share, so that if a company with 50p shares gives dividends of 10p during the year, it has given a dividend of 20 per cent. This is not used so much these days, but is helpful if looked at over a few years as it indicates how well the shareholders have been rewarded over time.

DIVIDEND COVER   This ratio is calculated in this way:

earnings per share / dividend per share

It is called dividend 'cover' because it shows how much of the profit is being taken out of the firm and whether the cost of the dividend is well secured. For instance, if a company has a dividend cover of 0.8, and the figures on which the ratio was calculated were: earnings £80,000, dividend £100,000, can you see a problem?

In a nutshell, if dividend cover is less than 1.00, the firm is paying some dividend out of reserves. Similarly, a very low ratio (e.g. 1.0 to 2.5) suggests either low earnings or a high pay-out level. Either way the firm may not be ploughing enough money back into the business.

Stock market profitability indicators

Where a company has its shares quoted on the stock market, another set of ratios can be calculated which uses the current market price of the shares. Although this figure is not usually quoted in the accounts, the ratios that can be calculated with it are important. Here is a brief description of the main ones.

Dividend yield

The formula for this ratio is:

(dividend per share × 100) / market price per share

If I buy a share at £3.60 and I receive a dividend of 18p, then the yield is 5 per cent, clearly an important thing to look at in taking an investment decision.

Price–earnings ratio (or p/e ratio)

This formula is:

market price per share / earnings per share

If a company has its shares valued at £3.60 and its EPS is 30p, then its p/e ratio is twelve times. The popularity of this ratio has declined in recent years with changes in the way tax is calculated. Moreover, there is no general agreement as to its utility. However, a very high p/e is a sign of a popular share – one with 'prospects'.

Earnings yield

This ratio is the p/e ratio turned upside down. It used to be popular and is calculated like this:

(earnings per share × 100) / market price per share

In the example we used for the p/e ratio, the earnings yield works out at 8.3 per cent. Some potential investors look for companies with a high earnings yield, since it may be a sign of a low-priced share. Profits are high in relation to the market's valuation of the firm, so there is a chance of a good dividend yield or a rise in the share price.

Return on shareholders' capital (ROSC)

Shareholders obtain their return in two ways, from dividends and from the growth in the value of the share itself. ROSC is therefore:

[(dividends + change in share price) / purchase price of share] × 100

For example, if I buy a share at £3.60 and receive a dividend of 18p, then sell the share for £4.14, the ROSC is 20 per cent. This is because the price of the share rose from £3.60 to £4.14 while I owned it, so its value increased by 54p, and by adding the dividend of 18p I obtained a total return of 72p, which is 20 per cent of the original investment.

Warning

With all the ratios that use current market prices, always remember that today's price is being compared with yesterday's profits – and there is no guarantee that profits will be as good next year.

What is an adequate return?

An adequate rate of return on capital (however measured) is vital for any business that wants to thrive. It is necessary for the following purposes:

- To reward the shareholders who have risked and tied up their money.
- To provide funds for the development and the growth of the business.
- To provide security for the employees and the lender's, as well as the firm's suppliers.
- To be able to pay for next year's goods and services at inflated prices, without reducing reserves.

There is no single percentage which serves as a yardstick for 'adequate'. However, there are some very general sources of information that may help:

- Look at the rate of interest that banks are offering. This is really a minimum rate of return and, the more risky the business, the higher the return should be.
- If you have a business of your own, you may be able to obtain some ratios about other firms in your industry or trade from the trade press or the trade association.
- The *Financial Times* and the magazines *Management Today* and *The Investors' Chronicle* all publish statistics of business performance.

The analysis of profitability and growth helps us to gain an appreciation of where the company stands in terms of its overall performance, since the measures we discussed are all common indicators of commercial success. It is, however, important to probe beneath the surface to see if there is any sign of weakness which may affect the future success of the firm and also to be able to identify the factors which have influenced the company in the past.

The main areas to investigate are the firm's financial strength, its assets, its financial structure and its operational efficiency.

CATEGORY 3: FINANCIAL STRENGTH

The third group of questions we identified on p. 79 which can be asked about a company relates to what I have called 'financial strength' and to what are sometimes described as 'financial health' measures. The answers to questions like this help us to decide whether the company is in danger of being short of money and of not being able to pay bills or meet debts. Several ratios are commonly calculated to do this job for us; some are called 'liquidity ratios' and others are known as 'financial cover ratios'.

EXERCISE

For instance, if you had £5 in your pocket, £50 in the bank and nothing else you could turn into money quickly, and you owed £100 to the electricity company which had to be paid by the end of the week, what words would you use to describe your financial situation?

Would it make any difference if you were going to receive £500 in wages at the end of the week?

You might well describe your position as desperate if no income was due, but where money was expected the situation could be described as embarrassing. In accountants' language 'there is a liquidity problem'. Accountants use two ratios to look at liquidity: the current ratio and the acid-test ratio.

The current (or working capital) ratio

The current ratio relates a firm's current liabilities to its current assets to indicate its ability at a certain point in time to pay off its immediate debts. It is calculated as:

current assets / current liabilities

What is a 'good' size for the current ratio? The answer is: it all depends on the company and how successful it is, what its record is like – looking at the same ratio over several years – and what is considered to be 'normal' for the industry.

Shops tend to have very low figures, because they do not tie up much money in current assets; there are neither debtors nor work in progress. Heavy engineering firms will usually have stocks of materials and finished goods as well as debtors and work in progress, and their current ratio will be very high by comparison. The current ratio for GEC was 1.92 at 31 March 1992, whereas the comparable figure for Tesco was 0.60 (at 28 February 1992).

The acid-test (or quick) ratio

There is a snag with the current ratio as a measure of liquidity, namely that stocks and work in progress may not easily be converted into money. In other words, they are relatively 'illiquid'. For example, GEC had about 20 per cent of its current assets tied up in either work in progress, or contracts in progress, i.e. incomplete construction work. None of these could be turned to cash quickly. If a firm is in a hurry to raise money, it may have to sell its stocks of materials and finished goods at less than their book value, so these elements in current assets are not usually considered to be liquid assets. In fact liquid assets are cash + debtors + short-term investments, and it is these that are available for paying off current liabilities. The ratio is therefore:

liquid assets / current liabilities

A very low acid-test ratio might be acceptable if current liabilities were very small relative to the amount of business being carried on (as in supermarkets), but there comes a point where being illiquid almost equates with insolvency – an inability to pay debts when due.

Interest cover ratio

The interest cover ratio looks at another aspect of the borrowing problem – namely, the ability of the firm to pay interest on the money it has borrowed. The ratio is calculated thus:

total profit / interest paid

Consider the relevant information for two similar-sized companies:

EXAMPLE

	Firm P (£000)	Firm Q (£000)
Operating profit + other income	650	750
Less: interest paid	130	300
Net profit before tax	520	450
Interest cover (times covered)	5.00	2.50

The problem for Firm Q is that if its profits fell and it still had the same amount of interest to pay, it could end up in a very embarrassing position; after paying the interest and tax, it might not have much left for the shareholders or to retain in the firm. A fall of 40 per cent in total profit for Firm P would leave it with pre-tax profits of £260.000 – a 50 per cent drop. On the other hand, a 40 per cent fall in total profit for Firm Q would leave it with pre-tax profits of only £150,000 – a 67 per cent drop.

You may see this ratio presented upside down and shown as a percentage, in which case it is called the 'income gearing ratio'.

Loan cover

Another aspect of the financial strength of a company is its ability to pay back borrowings. In particular, if a company wants to borrow for a medium- or long-term period, the lender usually seeks some kind of security for the loan. This applies to individuals as well as firms – if you want to borrow to buy a house, for example. With a company the ratio is:

fixed assets (at written-down book value) / all medium- and long-term debt

Here is an example of two companies with widely differing loan cover ratios. It is not difficult to see which could borrow more, assuming that profits and prospects are similar:

EXAMPLE

	Firm Y (£000)	Firm Z (£000)
Fixed assets	250	250
Loans (more than one year)	25	125
Loan cover	10.0	2.0

Firm Y has a very high ratio compared with Firm Z. Do you think that Z has the ability to borrow more than Y? Highly improbable!

CATEGORY 4: ASSETS

The next category of ratios to calculate helps us to understand a little more about where the company has tied up its money, and how well or badly it is using its assets.

EXERCISE: A CASE TO CONSIDER

There were once two small printing firms. At the end of the year both had tangible assets of £60,000. Firm A had made sales of £80,000 during the year, with a profit after tax of £8,000. Firm B had only managed a turnover of £60,000 and its profit after tax was £6,000. Both print shops were of similar size and of similar age and condition. What is the difference between the two?

The difference between them is that the second printing firm had a relatively low turnover, which points to poor asset utilisation. A ratio that measures this is:

sales / assets

and the figure for Firm A is 1.33 times, whereas for Firm B it is 1.00 times. In other words, firm A is turning over its assets faster than firm B; it is utilising its assets better.

An alternative ratio to express this idea is:

(assets/sales) × 1,000

The figures for the two firms are:

- firm A, £750;
- firm B, £1000.

This shows that firm A needs £750 of assets to generate £1,000 of sales, whereas firm B needs £1,000 of assets to generate £1,000 of sales. The neat thing about this particular ratio is that it can be used for all asset items:

(stocks/sales) × 1,000 +
(debtors/sales) × 1,000 =
(current assets / sales) × 1,000

and

(land and buildings / sales) × 1,000 +
(plant and machinery / sales) × 1,000 =
(fixed assets / sales) × 1,000

Also:

(current assets / sales) × 1,000 +
(fixed assets / sales) × 1,000 =
(total assets / sales) × 1000

Each of these asset utilisation ratios shows the amount of money tied up in the particular asset for every £1,000 of sales generated.

Below, you will see the asset ratios of a company over a two-year period. By comparing one year's ratios with another, you will very quickly be able to see where the company is not utilising its assets as well as before.

EXAMPLE

The Grand Manufacturing Co. Ltd

	Year 1 (£ per £1,000)	Year 2 (£ per £1,000)
Material stocks	100	100
Work in progress	20	25
Finished goods stock	40	42
Debtors	120	150
Current assets	280	317
Land and buildings	60	58
Plant and machinery	160	167
Fixed assets	220	225
Total assets	500	542

The ratios highlight the fact that several items are moving the wrong way – work in progress, finished goods and plant and machinery . However, the main cause of the poor situation is the very big increase in debtors, not in absolute terms but in relation to sales.

Other asset ratios

In addition to the ratios we have been looking at, there are some others which can make our analysis even better.

Debtors

debtors / sales × 365

This shows the average number of days customers take to pay up.

Materials stocks

materials stocks / cost of materials used × 365

This shows the average number of days' usage of materials in hand.

Finished goods stocks

finished goods stocks / production cost of goods made × 365

This ratio tells you how many days' sales equivalent there is in stock.

CATEGORY 5: FINANCIAL STRUCTURE

The ratios we have been looking at are fairly straightforward because they are describing and analysing asset structure.

The other side of the balance sheet – that relating to capital – is more complex, and in many ways more significant when it comes to evaluating risk. The important fact to establish is how much of the company's assets have been bought with equity capital and how much with borrowed money. There is a simple ratio to measure this:

debt/equity = the 'gearing' ratio

Here are sets of figures for three firms in the same line of business:

EXAMPLE

	Company A (£000)	Company B (£000)	Company C (£000)
Equity capital	600	400	300
Borrowed capital	400	600	700
Total capital (or total assets)	1,000	1,000	1,000
(Debt/equity) %	0.67	1.50	2.33

The profit and loss accounts for the three firms will look like this:

	A £	B £	C £
Trading profit	250	250	250
Less interest (at 9 %)	36	54	63
Profit before tax	214	196	187
(Profit/equity %)	35.7	49.0	62.3

It is clear, therefore that the firm with the highest gearing has the best return on equity and the firm that has borrowed least has the lowest return. You will, of course, remember the problem with a high level of borrowing that we discussed on p. 90 (the interest cover ratio); namely, if profits fall substantially, the firm with the highest level of borrowing is most at risk. So the message about gearing is:

High gearing is good for the shareholders in times of a high level of activity, but it is bad when things are not going so well.

There are other ways of calculating gearing and it is very difficult to generalise about what is an acceptable level of gearing. It depends on the company, its products, the market it's in, the state of the industry and the economy, and how much risk the owners and the directors of the firm are prepared to take. If they do not borrow and have a very low level of gearing, they are said to be 'risk–averse'.

CATEGORY 6: OPERATING EFFICIENCY

In the examples above, we assumed that the three firms were equally efficient. Naturally this does not happen all that often in reality, and it is important to find out why one company is better than another, or indeed why operating efficiency may have deteriorated from one year to another.

The starting point is usually the profitability ratio, which looks at the results of the firm at the trading level. What is then needed is some ratios that will explain how that level of profitability has been achieved and why it is different (either from the previous year or as against other firms).

The twin factors determining profitability

The level of profitability in any company is determined by two key factors. These are the overall utilisation of assets that wè have already seen and a very well-known concept – the 'profit margin on sales'.

The ratio that measures profit margins is

(trading profit / sales) × 100

and when calculated it shows just how much profit has been made from £100 of sales.

Below you will see the sales, operating profits and profit margins for two firms in the same business:

EXAMPLE

	Bond Street Ltd (£000)	Pavement Spiv Co. (£000)
Sales	400	800
Operating (trading) profit	60	60

The profit margin on Bond Street Ltd's operations is 15 per cent, whereas for Pavement Spiv Co. it is only 7.5 per cent. Both are making the same amount of profit, but the first firm is achieving its results on half the turnover. There are a variety of reasons why one company should have a higher profit margin than another and it is possible to get some clues by looking at the ratios relating to costs. You will remember that:

sales − costs = profit

Or:

costs + profit = sales

In the same way:

(profit/sales)% + (cost/sales)% = 100%

So a firm with a profit margin of 15 per cent of sales must have total costs of 85 per cent of sales.

Many cost ratios can be calculated, and listed below are some of the common cost items used to calculate these ratios – usually with sales (sometimes value added) as the common denominator.

- Cost of goods sold (and gross profit).
- Total wages.
- Distribution costs.
- Selling costs.
- Production costs.
- Overheads.

The main difficulty with cost ratios is that the information needed is not always given in the published accounts. Internally the figures should be available.

An overall picture

The three main ratios we have looked at are linked together logically and mathematically so that if you multiply the profit on sales ratio by the asset turnover ratio, you arrive at the profitability ratio:

profit/sales $\times$ sales/assets = profit/assets

HOW A BUSINESS WORKS

We can now come to some conclusions about the way any company operates. We have already seen what causes the profit/sales ratio to be high or low, and you also know when to expect a fast or slow turnover ratio.

Here are some figures:

EXAMPLE

	Profit/ sales	*Sales/ assets*	*Profit/ assets*
a jewellery shop	20%	1.00	20%
a successful supermarket chain	4%	4.00	16%
an unsuccessful heavy engineering company	7%	0.60	4.2%

a successful company making electronic
equipment   12%   1.50   18%

Not every combination of figures is possible, since it is very difficult for a firm to have both a very high profit margin on sales and a
very fast turnover of assets at the same time. This is because it is
impossible to be simultaneously labour-intensive and capital-
intensive. Moreover, a quality product with a high price and with a
correspondingly high profit margin is not likely to have the volume
of sales to give it a fast turnover of assets.

SUMMARY OF THE CHAPTER

■ Ratio analysis provides the key to interpreting accounting statements. The ratios were grouped into six categories – be sure that
you can name them and give some examples of each. There are, of
course, other ratios which can be used; but be wary of books and
articles that quote just a handful of ratios and pretend that nothing
else is needed – a great deal more is sought by people who are
actually going to invest time or money in a business.

■ Remember, too, that published accounts give limited information,
but internally all the information needed for effective management
should be available, and the relevant ratios should always be
presented.

12 *Factors affecting growth and success*

This chapter draws together the important ideas presented in this book, showing how an appreciation of the financial facts of business life is not an unnecessary burden, but provides a foundation for success.

WHY DOES A BUSINESS EXIST?

All business ventures, whether they are huge, like Ford or Shell, or tiny, like the corner shop, exist to satisfy someone or other. Large companies, with shares on stock markets, exist to satisfy a range of stakeholders to a greater or lesser degree. These stakeholders include shareholders, management, other staff, customers, suppliers, possibly lenders and even society as a whole. However, a small firm may exist just to keep the owner's family at a reasonable standard of living.

Survival is the minimum requirement of most firms. After that, 'satisfying' different needs is difficult to measure.

It is reasonable to assume that a shrinking, profitless, cash-short business is not going to satisfy many people for long, unless it has some very bright ideas in the pipeline. On the other hand, stakeholders will be relatively well satisfied with a company which has demonstrated growth over the years, in profits, dividends, market share and in its net worth, as well as a growth in its stock market value (where applicable), even when times are tough.

WHY DO COMPANIES GO BROKE?

At one level, a company either ceases to trade because the bank or other creditors stop it, or voluntarily ceases to trade and calls in the receivers or the administrators. In either case, action is taken because the firm is unable to pay its debts – or likely to be unable to pay in the near future. Why do firms get into this situation? There have been enough cautionary tales in the preceding chapters of this book to supply quite a long list of answers to this. The accounts of a company do not cause it to go broke. Rather, accounting information reveals what has gone wrong and there are two levels of cause:

- the accounting manifestation; and
- the root problem.

ACCOUNTING MANIFESTATION OF FAILURE

1 Too much working capital.
2 Insufficient working capital.
3 Too high interest charges.
4 Too much debt.
5 Over-high dividends.
6 No cash.
7 Making a trading loss.
8 No growth.
9 Selling parts of the firm at a loss.
10 Very poor profit margins.
11 Marginal profitability.

No one of these on its own is a cause of collapse, but when several appear together, the danger signs are there. Even so, they all have root causes and these can be summarised as:

1 Not selling enough.
2 Not selling at the right prices.
3 Not modernising.
4 No product development or research.
5 Buying useless assets.
6 Failure to control costs.
7 Failure to control working capital.
8 Reckless borrowing.
9 Having a cavalier dividend policy.

Perhaps to these should be added a *failure to invest in people.*

These things do not happen all at the same time, but if the trends are observed over two or three years, then it is often easy to identify trouble brewing, unless management does something drastic and takes corrective action.

Maybe you can add your own causes: some may be external, many will be internal, but the above nine factors, for whatever reason, are at the heart of all business failure (including those where fraud has been involved).

WHAT MAKES A SUCCESSFUL FIRM?

In contrast to failure, successful firms do all the opposite things to the nine deadly business sins just described. 'Good' firms sell enough of the right things, at sensible prices and at the right margin to be able to utilise their assets effectively. They control costs and working capital. They plough lots of profit back. Their borrowing is appropriate to their risk-exposure. We can see these virtuous features by looking at their key ratios over time and by the way the competition (and the 'City') views them.

COMPLETING THE PICTURE

Arguably, the most important single measure of business success is the *return on equity capital ratio.* This measures how effectively management has used the shareholders' money, and over time indicates whether the firm is making any kind of progress. At this level, the 'return' is the profit available to the shareholders – to take out of the business as a dividend or plough back to finance growth. The higher the return the greater the wealth creation – either directly to the owners – or indirectly by adding to the net worth of the firm. In the last chapter we discussed the two key elements that determine operating profitability – the profit on sales ratio and the turnover of assets. These can easily be linked to the return on equity capital ratio by introducing a gearing ratio into the equation:

$$\frac{\text{Net profit after tax}}{\text{Sales}} \times \frac{\text{Sales}}{\text{Assets employed}} \times \frac{\text{Assets employed}}{\text{Equity capital}} = \frac{\text{Net profit after tax}}{\text{Equity capital}}$$

A simple example will show that this equation can give you a quick picture of how a company arrived at its return on equity position:

EXAMPLE

	£million
Sales	24
Net profit after tax	3
Assets employed	20
Equity capital	12
Profit/sales(%)	12.5
Sales/assets	1.2
Gearing	1.67
Profit/equity(%)	25.0

Just how important the gearing part of the equation is, can be seen if you look at the difference between these two sets of ratios:

A: $12.0\% \times 1.00 \times 1.10 = 13.2\%$
B: $8.0\% \times 1.00 \times 2.50 = 20.0\%$

The second differs from the first for two reasons: it has a very high gearing and a lower profit margin on sales. The lower margin is to be expected because its higher gearing implies higher interest payments and so lower profits. But look at the final outcome: B is much more profitable as far as the shareholders are concerned. If all the profit was ploughed back, B would be growing – adding value for the shareholders – at a much faster rate than A. Clearly there is a greater risk; if there was a sudden downturn in trade B would suffer. But in a well-managed company such risks are also well-managed. In conclusion, therefore:

Creating wealth and adding shareholder value is determined by long-run growth and a high return on equity.

This in turn is determined by:

■ The size of the profit margin on sales.
■ The speed of asset turnover.
■ The level of gearing.

This book began by asking: why does a business exist? The answers are many, but all are underpinned with sound financial management and *every* manager is responsible in some part for ensuring that decisions with a financial consequence do have a sound base.

Further reading

Chartered Institute of Management Accountants (1991) *Management Accounting, Official Terminology*, London: CIMA.

Glautier, M.W.E. and Underdown, B. (1991) *Accounting Theory and Practice*, London: Pitman.

Hussey, Roger (1989) *Cost and Management Accounting*, London: Macmillan.

Knott, Geoffrey (1991) *Financial Management*, London: Macmillan.

Sizer, John (1991) *An Insight into Management Accounting*, new edition, Harmondsworth: Penguin.

Westwick, C.A. (1991) *How to Use Management Ratios*, Aldershot: Gower.